# WALKING WITH GARBO

# WALKING WITH
# GARBO

*Conversations and Recollections*

# RAYMOND DAUM
## EDITED AND ANNOTATED BY
# VANCE MUSE

HarperCollins*Publishers*

To Lillian Gish
*The Lady Who Sent
the Flowers*

Grateful acknowledgment is made for permission to reprint the following:

From "Our Footloose Correspondents: A Spanish Shawl for Miss Garbo" by E. W. Selsey, published in *The New Yorker*, April 23, 1938, © 1938, 1966 The New Yorker Magazine, Inc. Excerpted by special permission. All rights reserved.

From "Profiles: American Pro Tem" by Virgilia Peterson Ross, published in *The New Yorker*, March 7, 1931, © 1931, 1959 The New Yorker Magazine, Inc. Excerpted by special permission. All rights reserved.

Letters from Garbo from "Greta Garbo," a Swedish documentary produced by Aina Behring, written by Sven Broman and Ake Wihlney.

Photograph credits:

All photographs are from The Lester Glassner Collection except the following: on pages 53, 59, 74, 141, 223 from the Robert Dance Collection; on pages 71, 83, 125, 159 from the Clarence Brown Collection, the University of Tennessee, Knoxville; on pages 116, 124 from the Bettmann Archive; on page 129 from George Ogee; on page 165 courtesy *Vanity Fair,* copyright 1932 (renewed 1960) by Condé Nast Publications, Inc.; on page 179 from January 1991 *Mirabella.*

FIRST EDITION

DESIGNED BY JOEL AVIROM

Library of Congress Cataloging-in-Publication Data

Daum, Raymond W.
    Walking with Garbo : conversations and recollections / Raymond Daum ; edited and annotated by Vance Muse.— 1st ed.
        p.   cm.
    ISBN 0-06-016492-1
    1. Garbo, Greta, 1905–1990.   2. Motion picture actors and actresses—Sweden—Biography.   I. Garbo, Greta, 1905–1990.   II. Muse, Vance, 1949– .
III. Title.
PN2778.G3D38   1991
791.43′028′092—dc20                              90-55925
[B]

91  92  93  94  95  DT/CW
10  9  8  7  6  5  4  3  2  1

# CONTENTS

*B*efore meeting Raymond Daum I knew his friend only from the distance that made her most comfortable with human beings—the distance that separates an audience from a movie screen. Along with the whole world, it seemed, I thought Greta Garbo was remarkably beautiful, that she spoke and moved just as beautifully, and I was also struck by how she might have been a contemporary: There is nothing long-ago or faraway about her appeal. I liked the way Garbo could seem at once passionate and indifferent, and I admired her for having the sense and the courage to say goodbye to Hollywood and to all of us. Sometimes I wondered what Garbo was thinking in her historic recline: Was she reeling from the impact she had made in her fleeting career? Half a century after her disappearance from the movies, the name and image still summon up her legend—as an artist, as an immigrant making her way in an industry run by men, and as a timeless beauty.

The Garbo that Raymond Daum knew is some of the things we imagine she would be, but she also is inquisitive and witty, and ever so sensitive and real: shaken by the deaths of her friends, proud of her modest way in the kitchen, afraid of friendly knocks at her door. Hearing her go on about sunshine and fresh air, you expect to find this commonsensical woman tilling land or raising sheep somewhere. But in the next sigh she is her urbane self, and totally aware of her exalted position. Her moment-by-moment accounts of a day approach the Warholian—Garbo is that good at making the quotidian seem absolutely important. Her report from a December afternoon wandering the ghostly streets of New York is riveting; her description of a squat little man selling hot dogs heartbreaking. Throughout, Garbo refers to herself in the masculine—as a boy, a young man, a bachelor. As she explained to Daum, "I think of myself as mankind—because 'girl' sounds so silly, so I always say, 'boy.' "

If you listen carefully you'll hear clues to a life story still so veiled in mystery that it can never be definitively told. Moving back and forth in time, between Stockholm, Hollywood, and New York, Garbo recalls the adult responsibilities forced upon her as a girl growing up on the grim edges of Stockholm; the hope that carried her into New York Harbor; the failed dreams of her mentor, Mauritz Stiller; her battles with Louis B. Mayer. Her words reveal the reluctant pride she takes in her legacy on film, and her delight in such simple things as walking through a light snowfall or bantering with a shopkeeper.

Behind the wisdom, the humor, and the strangeness of her commentary is the poignant desire of a woman at odds with her extraordinary fame and with her isolation. "I've always wanted two lives," she says at one point. "One for the movies and one for myself." In intimate conversation, Garbo now brings us a little closer to the one life she did have. Garbo thought before she spoke, and she spoke slowly, as if meditating on each syllable. As you read her words, set here in larger type, keep Garbo's soothing, smoky alto in your ear. First heard on the screen in 1930, the voice can still bring you forward in your seat.

—VANCE MUSE

# A Portrait in Conversation

I was dreading this occasion and feeling blue as I stepped from the cab at the corner of York and Seventy-second Street on the afternoon of Thursday, November 15, 1990. Across the windows of Sotheby's was an enormous placard with the initials 'G. G.,' a facsimile of Greta Garbo's distinctive signature, which she used to sign her personal notes. It was a shock—almost like attending the funeral that had never been held. (No public announcement of her burial had been made, and it was known only that she had been cremated.) Hundreds of people were lined up along the sidewalk, barricaded by New York police.

I walked to the side door and told the guard there that I had been personally invited by Garbo's family, the Reisfields, and I was shown quickly upstairs to the private viewing room, which overlooks the auction hall. Garbo's handsome niece, Mrs. Gray Reisfield, greeted me warmly, and introduced me to her husband and four children. I thanked her for the invitation and made my way to the auction hall.

The room was in a frenzy: television and film cameras and recording apparatus were clustered to one side, and auctioneers issued announcements through loudspeakers. Every seat was filled, the audience a mix of old and young, shabby and rich, each there for a different reason.

It was macabre seeing Miss G's precious possessions being paraded forward into the spotlights in front as the auctioneer gave the lot a number. Feeling uneasy, like an intruder on her privacy, I turned and headed for the exit.

She was gone, out of our lives. It was my first hard realization that the power of her presence no longer existed. In the cab driving away, I could almost hear her whispering, "Imagine! All my beautiful things in the hands of strangers." It was the ultimate violation of her legendary privacy, yet she would have been amused and secretly flattered had she known that the auction would net over twenty million dollars, her elegant furniture and paintings by Bonnard and Renoir and what she called the "staring face" pictures by Alexei Von Jawlensky. Now, even the symbols of the "Divine Garbo" were being scattered, leaving only the mystery of her life.

After she left Hollywood and settled in New York, Greta Garbo remained reclusive, famously so, as she had been almost since the day of her arrival in the United States from Sweden in July of 1925. But she was not the complete shut-in that most imagined her to be. Garbo could easily be coaxed out to a favorite restaurant (the Swedish Three Crowns, or Maude Chez Elle), or to a matinee, or to a small dinner party. She was frequently spotted as she darted in and out of the city's airports, on her way to and from Europe or California. And she was a familiar, shrouded apparition on the city streets, walking by herself or with various companions—Gayelord Hauser, Jessica Dragonette, Eric de Rothschild-Goldschmidt, Cecil Beaton, and George Schlee. If Garbo was a hermit, then she was a very visible one—as someone quipped, "a hermit about town."

On a snowy New Year's Day of 1963, Ruth Ford and Zachary Scott invited me to one of their afternoon "Irish Coffees" at their apartment in the Dakota. Because of my work as a film and television producer at the United Nations, I had come to know a lot of people in the international film world, some of whom were there that day, along with Elia Kazan, Norman Mailer, Ned Rorem, and Kenneth Clark. The party was candlelit, with curtains drawn across windows over West Seventy-third Street, and as I made my way in the half-light, I suddenly noticed that sitting on a hassock in the center of the library was Greta Garbo. She was dressed in light gray trousers and a pale violet turtleneck. George

Schlee, the husband of designer Valentina but Garbo's constant companion, stood next to her. They were sipping vodka, and there was a reserved hush in the room around them.

Tammy Grimes, who at the time was appearing on Broadway in *High Spirits,* whispered to me, "Isn't this remarkable? A room full of adults, and not one of us will approach her." It was true—the guests had carefully left her to herself. I would have done the same, but it was too rare an opportunity not to take the chance of meeting her.

I knew George Schlee through mutual friends, including Eustace Seligman [his and Garbo's business advisor], a tremendously charming, erudite man. I went over to say hello. As I had hoped, the introduction was made, and Garbo smiled and offered a firm handshake. When Schlee mentioned that I worked for the United Nations, she made room on the hassock and said, "Sit down, Mr. Daum. And, Schleeski, get me another vodka."

She was made up lightly but carefully: pink lip rouge, mascara accenting long eyelashes, a pastel polish on the nails. She looked immaculate and gave off an aura of freshness. I hadn't anticipated the enchantment of Garbo's eyes and voice, which lingered long after that meeting. Her eyes always remained on those of the person to whom she was speaking; and in fact she had always taken stock of the personality of anyone she met by the look of his eyes and the tone of his voice. I realized that she was not at ease in this room, surrounded by so many people, and that she had relied on her friend to provide an island of sanctuary for her on the hassock.

Here I was at her side—the ultimate thrill for the starstruck son of a Los Angeles building contractor and member of the mayor's city council. My father in his youth had built sets at Paramount in the silent movie days, and the backlots were my playgrounds. For me, then and now, Garbo personified the glamour and magic of the movies.

On that unforgettable New Year's Day in New York, Garbo surprised me by asking a lot of questions about my work, though her interest wasn't so much in what I did as where I did it. She told me that she had windows facing the UN, that she walked by there almost every day and had always wondered what it was like inside. I told her a little about the organization and mentioned that I lived nearby, on Beekman Place, and she seemed pleased to hear that we were neighbors on the East Side. We talked that way for a half-hour or so, about small things, and as Garbo and George prepared to slip out without a word to the other guests or to their hosts, I offered to give her a tour of the UN.

It wasn't until five months later, though, on May 16, that my office telephone rang and I heard George saying, "She'd like to come today." I instantly knew whom he meant, and at three o'clock that afternoon, he brought Garbo around in his black Humber limousine. I met them at the main Delegates Entrance, and Garbo removed her sunglasses as she stepped inside the lobby of the building. That was the only time I ever saw Garbo in a skirt—a gray pleated one, which she wore with a navy blazer. George waited in the Delegates Lounge—Garbo explained that he was suffering from lumbago (a word she always used to describe her own back pain)—and she and I set off walking. She had supplied herself with Kent cigarettes, but had lost her lighter and asked me for matches later in the lounge when we were having drinks.

The first thing that caught Garbo's notice was the expanse of blue carpet in all the corridors. When I told her it was a gift from the United Kingdom, she had an odd lament: "Imagine all those English girls working like mad at their looms—and imagine how little they were paid for their labor."

Moving along a corridor, we passed a few blinking, staring people, and I hoped she hadn't heard their gasps of recognition. When one woman made a nervous approach with pen and pad, I explained to her that it was Miss Garbo's rule never to give autographs. Garbo thanked me and apologized for refusing the request. That was the only interruption of our tour, and after an hour or so we collected Schlee, and I saw them out.

A few weeks later, I saw Garbo again, at a cocktail party at the Schlees' apartment. Garbo arrived with her friend Cecile de Rothschild, and before leaving I suggested that we three take in a movie sometime soon. The next day was October 30, and I sent Garbo a pumpkin and a bouquet from our neighborhood florist and reiterated my invitation. I still have the typewritten note she wrote on Halloween, thanking me. About our movie date, she was noncommittal, but promised to call soon. Her note was signed with a faint but large "G. G."

Almost a year passed before I contacted Garbo again, and the occasion was a sad one: George Schlee had died suddenly while in Paris with Garbo. My telephone number was on the note of condolence I sent her, and Garbo called a few days later. She seemed genuinely anxious to talk to me and asked if she could come for a visit. I said yes, of course, and she arrived less than an hour later. She and George had been inseparable, and his widow, Valentina, had now turned against Garbo. At one point, Garbo sighed deeply, and her eyes filled with tears. "Everyone I love dies." I knew then our friendship was to be genuine, and realized how much it meant to her that George and I had been good friends.

Alone for the first time with Garbo, I seemed to be really seeing her, the public facade—the floppy hats, sunglasses, upraised hand hiding her face—gone. She casually passed off a glowing compliment with an easy laugh. Her voice, low and resonant, was modulated with aristocratic English vowels, a sound one never forgot. A gold signet ring graced her left hand, the gift of a noble. Did the ring bear the Rothschild or the Bernadotte crest? She would never tell me.

After many more of these impromptu visits, she suddenly rang up one day and said: "Let's trot."

She wanted me to meet her at the corner of First Avenue and Fifty-second Street for one of her walks around town. I knew Garbo was a great walker—everyone in New York knew that, for it was the only time they saw her—and I was thrilled to be invited along. I'm not sure where we went that first day, but over the weeks, months, years, it seems we hiked the length and breadth of Manhattan.

In her trenchcoats, hats, and dark glasses, Garbo went about mostly undisturbed, though during one of our more ambitious walks, we realized that a man was following us through Washington Square. We ducked into a pub, but so did our pursuer, and over a glass of sherry, Garbo whispered to me, "I heard him say my name." The man remained a polite distance across the room, but when he turned away for a moment, we bolted out a side door onto teeming Bleecker Street. The incident made her more uncomfortable than displeased. I think she even sympathized with people who trailed after her, since she, too, was given to great curiosity during our rambles. "Often I just go where the man in front of me is going," she once said jokingly.

We talked about everything but her past and her career. "Don't ever ask me about the movies," she once cautioned me. "Especially why I left them." I never did ask her about her films directly—none of her friends dared to—but often I dropped hints or tried to say something leading, alluding to her years in Hollywood, hoping to hear something about the mystery of her past. But as I learned, Garbo would reveal herself to me on her own terms and in her own time.

And so it went for "Miss G" and "Mr. Daum" (as we addressed each other) into the 1980s, always picking up where we left off, after Garbo's stays in California and Switzerland and sojourns to the Caribbean, and my various travels and graduate study at the University of Hawaii. In 1983, I became a curator in Theater Arts at the Harry Ransom Humanities Research Center at the University of Texas at Austin. Garbo did not like the idea of my departure from New York. "So, Mr. Daum, you're leaving us," she said. "Yes, you are, you're moving out of the neighborhood."

But I now had a doctorate in Communications from Columbia University, and the Texas offer was a good one. The Harry Ransom Center in Austin is renowned for its collection of theater arts and twentieth-century British manuscripts and has also begun acquiring an important Hollywood collection, centered around the David O. Selznick Archive. At my urging, Gloria Swanson placed her collection of papers and memorabilia with the university. The Ransom Center has also acquired such diverse archives as actor Zachary Scott's (from his widow Ruth Ford) and, in 1990, Steve Martin's.

Writing from Austin, I now approached Garbo in a professional context. Would she consider leaving her papers with the University of Texas, so that film scholars and biographers could study her life and career? I knew she had a file cabinet in a back room of the apartment on East Fifty-second Street, and I imagined that it contained treasures—Garbo's original contracts with MGM; notes from such directors as George Cukor and Ernst Lubitsch; movie stills; portraits by Clarence Bull and Ruth Harriet Louise; even scripts that Garbo might have scribbled on in Swedish.

But Garbo claimed that whatever she might have saved from the "old days" was unimportant. She added matter-of-factly that she would toss it all into a fire one day. "It'll all be burned up," she said, adding that she wished to be cremated after her death. And, after Garbo died, her survivors say, the file cabinet was found to be empty.

Though I could not convince her to let the university have her papers, she and I kept in touch and saw each other on my occasional trips to New York. But, slowly, as her health declined, we fell out of touch, and Garbo stopped answering my notes. As other friends had learned, when you left Garbo's orbit, she drifted away from you.

During the years of my friendship with Garbo, I had helped launch at Columbia University the "American Biography Project," an oral history archive that contains interviews I conducted with a wide range of people in the arts—Lillian Gish, Stephen Sondheim, the architect Wallace Harrison, Alfred Hitchcock, Mary Rodgers, Arthur Laurents—and had, as a result, developed a good ear for minutiae.

Shortly after Garbo and I had become walking companions, I began taking down our conversations. The model for my methodology came from reading Garson Kanin's description of his recordings of his private conversations with Somerset Maugham. Kanin wrote of ". . . events that I took great care to preserve— always putting down his words as soon after our meetings as possible." I would do the same with Garbo, not originally intending to write about her, but simply to savor the things she said and the wonderful way she said them.

Often after my visits with "Miss G," I would return home and repeat what she had said into my tape recorder. I used it also for an answering machine for the phone in those days, and I never erased Garbo's long rambling messages, or the fragments of my telephone conversations with that spell-binding voice. What she gave me were her thoughts, her philosophy, not explanations of her past. But, every now and then, she yielded to temptation and offered fragments of her experiences in the old California days.

In 1985, on the occasion of Garbo's eightieth birthday, I was contacted by the *New York Daily News* to write an article about her. The manuscript I prepared was a reminiscence of our conversations, her thoughts just as she conveyed them to me. I wanted her to know how much they had meant to me, our talks and walks. So I wrote to her, informing her about the *News* article and sent her the preface and chapter outlines of the book I was writing—to be called *Double Image,* promising to respect the richness of our friendship. She never responded, but intimate friends of Garbo later told me that she "even liked the idea of Mr. Daum's book." From that unpublished manuscript, *Walking with Garbo* has emerged.

Early in 1989, I heard from Vance Muse at *Life* magazine in New York. A special Hollywood issue was in the works, and, at the first story meeting, someone had muttered, "God, if we could get Garbo...." Editors have been saying that since 1928 when Garbo gave her last full-length interview. But Muse, whom I had met when he visited the Harry Ransom Center to research an article for *House & Garden,* knew I might have something for *Life.*

Excerpts of my conversations with Garbo from *Double Image* research were readied for publication in *Life,* but again, before proceeding, I and the editors wrote to Garbo telling her about the magazine feature and asking for her participation—not with any real hope of a response, but as a courtesy to her. Garbo was silent, even after the issue of the magazine was hand-delivered to her door and appeared on newsstands. The enthusiastic response to the article, called "Garbo Talks—a little," became another reason to pursue my plans of writing—not a biography, really, but a memoir of a friendship, a self-portrait made in her own words. Before I proceeded with a book, I apprised Garbo of my plans to publish. Again, she remained silent.

In fall of 1989, Vance Muse joined me as a researcher, editor, and annotator for HarperCollins's publication of *Walking with Garbo,* and work began in spring of 1990.

Only a few weeks later, on Easter Sunday of 1990, the sad news rang out. Garbo was dead, at eighty-four.

My times with Garbo had always been quiet, as is my celebration of her in these pages. A meeting with Garbo was always an event. As she entered a room, she presented a striking figure, even in later years. Garbo had a noble head, honey-colored skin, clean salt-and-pepper hair in bangs, and the weathered face of an outdoor woman, lined with age and offset by sad and searching blue-green eyes. She was taller than might be expected, five feet seven, and at 110 pounds, she remained boyishly slim.

On her visits, her decisions to leave were always unpredictable. A quick nod of the head signaled an end to the relaxed conversation we had shared—nothing especially profound, but sprinkled amply with good-natured laughter. "Well, well, well," she would say, concernedly, "look at the time. I should have gone home ages ago." She would put on her coat, not wishing to be helped, and, with a quick kiss on the cheek, she would go, leaving the impression that she was keeping to a tight schedule. In reality she had nothing more pressing than a solitary evening in her spacious fifth floor apartment, watching television, cooking for herself, and dining alone.

After she had gone, an impression of privacy, even secrecy remained. Despite our camaraderie, I understood that she tended to hide behind her conversation. The following enigmatic comment—which I always took to refer to George Schlee—may be as close as she ever came to revealing the deep secrets of her life.

"I'll tell you something—and I don't know why I said it in French, but I did:

> Dans quelque jours, il sera l'anniversaire de la douleur que ne me quitte pas, que ne me quitte pas pour la reste de ma vie."
> [In a few days it will be the anniversary of the sadness that never leaves me, will never leave me for the rest of my life.]

For years, I have privately treasured the gift of Garbo's words to me (which appear in larger print in this book), and they still provide instant and vivid mementoes of our magical walks together. I am happy to be able to share them now and introduce the woman I knew—so astute, warm, funny, and completely herself.

How I miss hearing that voice bid me goodbye with "Arrivi-derci" or its Swedish equivalent, "Adjö". But as she does in her films, I hope she will also live on in *Walking with Garbo*, my tribute to her, my neighbor, and my friend.

—RAYMOND DAUM

# 1 NEW YORK

Preceding page: *The inauspicious arrival. Garbo and her mentor, Mauritz Stiller, come to America.*

New York in the summer can be so horrid that you can't go out. One thinks one is going to die. And we're supposed to be images of God, living in clean . . . Well, it's insane.

It said in the paper today that it's the cleanest day or week that it has been in some time, because they're doing something about the air pollution from one factory, some bloody industrial business here. I never see anything in the paper, or I look in the paper and don't know what's in it—so I'm astonished that I saw that. Imagine, if one industry can foul up existence for all these thousands of people—that's pretty terrible, isn't it? They ought to remove them from the city. It can all be improved by using another kind of fuel, but however it's done, it seems incredible that the poor people have been harping on it for ten years or more, hoping that something would happen. And it's one industry, one single industry, that contributes such a large amount of the air pollution. The strife of humankind is really unfathomable, especially in New York.

The amazing thing is I don't have to be here in this fantastic filth and unpardonable climate. I could live anywhere. The few people I know in this world say, "How can you stand living in New York?" There was a woman coming through from California, on her way to Europe, and it was muggy, unbelievably hot, and I saw her for a minute and she said, "How can you stand living in this hell?" I could be living where they make up fresh loaves of bread and you look up at the trees, at the little birdies. I don't want to be here, it's abnormal.

I first came here when I was a very young boy. I didn't like it particularly, but it was exciting.

Now, actually, New York is the only home I have.

The city was not at all welcoming when Garbo arrived there in the summer of 1925, when she was nineteen years old. By her side was her director, Mauritz Stiller, twice her age and closer to her than anyone in the world. Each had a rare and wonderful prize in hand—a contract with Metro-Goldwyn-Mayer, which Stiller had negotiated in a face-to-face meeting with Louis B. Mayer, the studio's chief of production. Stiller was a familiar name to American filmmakers, and Garbo, unknown in this country, must have felt like his appendage, a tag-along. But recalling their approach to New York Harbor, she sounded like a wide-eyed maiden on a fantastic voyage: "When we saw the Statue of Liberty, lots of people screamed. They were from New York City and you felt it with them. I began to have the strange feeling of looking forward to things I had never seen." It was July 6, a Monday, and a horrid eighty-seven degrees out. To a delicate Northerner, the heat was withering.

It seems that Garbo had enjoyed her first transatlantic crossing, on the S.S. *Drottningholm,* a Swedish steamer that had taken ten days to cross from Göteborg. "Oh, that was marvelous, on the ocean," she later told *Photoplay.* "I would love to do that over and over." She said she did little else but take long walks around the deck, gaze at the horizon for hours at a time, and play shuffleboard (though she didn't know the word for it: "that game where you push things back and forth"). As for company, there was only Stiller, and "a tiny boy, little Tommy. I wanted so madly to give him cakes. But he had never eaten cakes. His mother and father were very careful."

But the truth may be that Garbo and Stiller passed the time with a small party of fellow film artists on board, among them

Erich Pommer, the German producer, on his way to Paramount with the vacationing Pola Negri, the "gypsy from Warsaw" whose most recent film, *Forbidden Paradise,* had been directed by Ernst Lubitsch. Also on board was the distinguished German actor Emil Jannings, who would win accolades for his portrayal of the pitiful professor ruined by his lust for Marlene Dietrich in *The Blue Angel.* All were familiar with Stiller and the protégée he had introduced to European audiences in *The Saga of Gösta Berling;* perhaps, in the ship's first-class lounge, they all offered toasts to one another's good fortune in Hollywood. But whatever festive moments Garbo and Stiller might have had on the trip over, their private conversations are what one now yearns to hear. Did they regret their decision to leave Sweden? Drill each other on English phrases? Was the master constantly grooming his pupil as they headed west? Stiller may have felt confident about the future, but Garbo, still so dependent on him, had less reason to.

She at least could know that she would have some financial security. Her first contract with MGM would bring her $18,200 per year—more than $139,000 in 1991 dollars. It was a small fortune, even by Hollywood standards: A year earlier, Joan Crawford had signed on as a nonfeatured player at Metro for $75 per week. Garbo was eager to get to work and start sending money home to Stockholm. She had resolved to stay in America for only one year, intending to return to work in European cinema. "Time passes quickly," she'd told her family when they saw her off at the railroad station for the first leg of her journey. "People do not know what it means to my people when somebody goes to America," Garbo said a year later. "There is always much crying—a feeling that they will never come back to their own country and their own people."

Stiller had trusted that he and Garbo would be met at the dock in New York by studio brass and by reporters and photographers. But on that muggy afternoon the greeting committee consisted of a single MGM hand, Hubert Voight, a man of Swedish descent who could speak the language; and a freelance photographer, James Sileo. To feed his charges, get them settled, and show them a good time that evening, Voight had a ten-dollar expense account (not extravagant, but not a dismal sum, either, when orchestra seats to a Broadway musical cost about three dollars, and half that amount bought a midtown table d'hôte luncheon). Howard Dietz, head of MGM's New York publicity department, did not turn out for Garbo and Stiller, nor did any studio executive. (Dietz, who created MGM's roaring-lion logo, was a real presence in New York; also an occasional lyricist, he had a dozen shows to his credit, including Jerome Kern's *Dear Sir* and *Poppy* starring W. C. Fields.)

While news photographers swarmed at the foot of the gangplank for the disembarking "Polish sensation," Pola Negri, Garbo and Stiller went through their studied motions for the one man pointing a camera at them. In the historic photograph, the director and his actress are standing side by side, leaning against the ship's railing. With his ankles crossed, and her right leg casually kicked behind her, they seem abundantly self-assured, about to take the town by storm. They are dressed rather alike, in gray checked suits: hers with a low-slung belt, his with a vest. He is wearing a jaunty racing cap, pulled down not so far as to hide his prominent brow; she is in a stylish, off-white cloche. Garbo is smiling and so is Stiller, but we can read the mood as forced: They are strangers in a strange land, they are scared, and they are disappointed by the tenor of their welcome. Captioned "Foreign Star Arrives," the photograph ran in only one of New York's fourteen dailies, the *Evening Graphic* (and one of the least read, with a circulation of 97,000 to the *Daily News*'s one million). The tabloid, which some tagged the "Pornographic," was currently running a cash-prize contest for "The Most Perfect Man and Woman."

Except for news of Calvin Coolidge, the Brooklyn Dodgers, and a bootlegger shoot-out in the South, the *New York Times* of July 6, 1925, resonates in a weirdly contemporary way: Mayoral candidates charged corruption in city government; blown girders on the Williamsburg Bridge stopped BMT trains and automobile traffic for three hours during the Fourth of July holiday weekend; clergymen decried a sharp increase in divorce. An antifur campaign was launched against fashion designers and manufacturers, "to reduce the unnecessary slaying of animals." But the big topic was the heat and how to beat it. Department stores and dress shops had installed oscillating electric fans to attract shoppers. Parasols were no longer in fashion, but brightly colored "sun umbrellas" were, available at Saks for $4.25. Weber & Heil-broner stores advertised men's "Palm Beach Suits" for $16.50—just the thing "when the sun beats down and the pavement begins to ooze." Straw chapeaux, "worn by fashionable New York women returning from abroad," were on sale for $3.50 at Lord & Taylor, and a Fifth Avenue import shop offered "cool Flowered Chiffons" for $55.00.

Garbo and Stiller were put at the Commodore Hotel on Forty-second Street, next to Grand Central. Once inside her stultifyingly hot room, Garbo promptly shed her clothes and drew a tub of cold water. "I could not get my breath," she told *Photoplay*, describing a bathing ritual that she would practice for the next two months. "I went from my bedroom to my bathroom to my room again. I used almost all of the water in New York City." Her spirits sagged in the heat and her hair frizzed. She could not get comfortable, or summon the energy to keep in touch with those back home. "See, I kept my word not to write," she finally wrote in an apologetic letter to Lars Saxon, a friend in Stockholm.

Stiller, who managed always to look sharp, worked at his typewriter in his room down the hall from Garbo's, pounding out story ideas and notes to Metro president Nicholas Schenck, who remained unavailable. Hadn't his and Garbo's employment with the studio commenced? Hadn't they been told to hurry over? Metro's offices were not far away, at 1540 Broadway, and an angry Stiller began showing up unannounced, demanding two things (loudly and mostly in Swedish): a meeting with producers and a screen test for Garbo. As Garbo languished in her tub, she apparently began to feel some dismay toward his behavior. "I have not appreciated the way Stiller has been so difficult, making trouble and causing delays here," she said in her letter to Lars Saxon.

I'm going nowhere for supper, but you should. If you have a bourgeois life, with a wife and five children, you can't, but you're not living that way, so go out. It's normal to want to go out. But if you want to go out, do it the way it's being done.

A person like me has no business being in New York. The word fun, I don't recognize. I go to bed with the chickens. I'm not a night person. If I'm out anywhere, which is very rare, I'm home before seven. There are so many things to do in New York, and if you don't do them, why sit here? I'm sure it's better to participate than to say no to everything. I've gotten myself in this rut and it's hard to get out once you're in it. Don't get in it, that's my advice.
New York belongs to the people who belong here.

It is hard to imagine two people more out of sync with the prevailing gaiety of Prohibition-era New York than Garbo and Stiller. Even to these veterans of European bohemia, the city must have been an intimidating free-for-all, with its high-voltage marquees along the Great White Way, burlesque-house barkers, beep-beeping Model-Ts and taxicabs, and shouting newsboys. In the jazzy interlude between the Great War and the Great Depression, the rush to be fast and clever was on—in print and in pictures, on stage and on the air, and at parties. "It was the twenties,"

*Garbo's first glimpse of Times Square, 1925.*

Dorothy Parker said from the relative calm of the following decade. "You had to be a smarty-pants." In speakeasies all over town, the talk was of *The New Yorker,* founded in February of 1925, and of *The Great Gatsby,* which had been published in May. People were laughing at the silliest things. The Marx Brothers were appearing on Broadway in *Monkey Business,* and one of Hal Roach's latest "Our Gang" comedies was titled *Mary, Queen of Tots.* Noel Coward's *Hay Fever* was announced for the fall season. Fifth Avenue and Tuxedo Park hostesses entertained their guests by inviting Ruth Draper to perform "The Italian Lesson" and other monologues—many of them caustic portraits of Fifth Avenue and Tuxedo Park hostesses.

To its Hall of Fame that year, *Vanity Fair* named Fanny Brice, "because, from the humblest beginnings on the East Side of New York, she came to be acclaimed as the best comedian on the musical comedy stage and because she is a financial genius of high rank"; and Al Jolson, "because, without aspiring to art, he is one of the great artists of the American theatre [and] because he is an important factor in the gaiety of nations." The magazine also nominated Sweden's erudite, tennis-swell of a prince, Gustavus Adolphus, "because he is the most popular royal visitor to these shores since the Prince of Wales."

Waiting for MGM to call, Garbo and Stiller did take in some theater, and one is tempted to call it a fateful season. If Garbo had known that she would make her talking-picture debut in Eugene O'Neill's *Anna Christie,* would she have dashed over to the Ambassador Theatre to see the playwright's *Desire Under the Elms,* with Walter Huston? Katharine Cornell and Leslie Howard were starring in *The Green Hat,* which Garbo would film as *A Woman of Affairs.* And there was Ina Claire—who would marry John Gilbert and play Garbo's rival in *Ninotchka*—appearing as a nutty dowager robbed of her jewels in *The Last of Mrs. Cheyney.* "The Snappiest and Cleanest Musical in Town," according to the ads, was a twirl of cotton candy called *My Girl.* But all that is known for certain of Garbo and Stiller's theatergoing is that they saw the *Ziegfeld Follies* at the New Amsterdam Theatre (Fanny Brice was not appearing, but W. C. Fields and Will Rogers were). Later asked what she had enjoyed about musical comedy, Garbo said, "I liked watching the American people." Such entertainments were perfect fare for non-English-speaking visitors, particularly these two, whose need for diversion had grown acute.

In 1964, film producer Bill Frye, an acquaintance from California, took Garbo to a Saturday matinee of *Funny Girl.* "We slipped in just as the show began," says Frye, "but during intermission someone said, 'There's Garbo.' It was pandemonium. People swarmed around us, pointing at her. She actually was quite gracious, but it made her so uncomfortable, she said we just had to go. I said, 'G.G., if we try to push our way out of the Winter Garden it'll make things worse.' People eventually calmed down, Garbo too. We had wonderful seats. Streisand was singing, and Garbo loved it."

Less than a decade later, Garbo had withdrawn severely. Catching up with her on a midtown street one afternoon in 1972, Tennessee Williams offered Garbo tickets to a performance of his play, *Small Craft Warnings.* "How wonderful," she said. "Thank you. I don't go out anymore."

New York only matters to people who are really participating and who are really New Yorkers. They have lots of things to do here. I don't go to what is called exciting . . . the theaters, concerts, the things—I don't go to them.

I don't even go to the cinema. Every day it's out there working like mad and I never go near it. They're all there, all the movies, but I don't go.

Have you seen one of those filthy movies? I haven't. I don't know what it's all about, but I must say I don't care. I can't figure out what it would prove, what it would alter, or what it would further in any way at all. If I were walking past the theater, maybe I'd go in if the spirit moved me. But if there's a line, I certainly wouldn't.

Stranded in the moviegoing capital of the world, Garbo and Stiller could appraise American film (including their new studio's contributions) at a time when the industry was burgeoning. The number of movie theaters in the United States was nearing twenty thousand, some of them opulent pleasure palaces, with programs that included singers and dancers and novelty acts. (Going to the movies also provided escape from the heat; the Rivoli, on Broadway at Forty-ninth Street, promised patrons "pure refrigerated air ... your ideal combination of Canadian Rockies, Maine woods, and Atlantic City.") At the Capitol, MGM's flagship theater in Times Square, two coming attractions were advertised that summer of 1925: *The Big Parade,* a World War I drama that would make John Gilbert a major star; and "that Phantom of the Opera," Lon Chaney, in *The Unholy Three,* a murder mystery set in a circus sideshow. The impresario Major Edward Bowes sold patrons a full evening's divertissements, including a ballet called "Gallop," featuring a prima ballerina known as Mademoiselle Gambarelli and her caparisoned corps; and a recital by Caroline Andrews, coloratura, backed by the Capital Grand Orchestra and Chorus. A dog act or a balloon artist might have opened the show. Movie theaters in Sweden never offered anything so spectacular or so silly.

The choice of films was enormous, from a Tom Mix western and a new Rin Tin Tin adventure to Norma Shearer in *A Slave to Fashion* and Douglas Fairbanks's latest, *Don Q, Son of Zorro.* Opening in August was Erich von Stroheim's bizarre *Merry Widow,* with Mae Murray and John Gilbert (Stiller admired the controversial director, who was later run out of Hollywood for his temperament and extravagance). Lewis Stone, who would make seven pictures with Garbo, was appearing with Nita Naldi in *The Lady Who Lied.* And showing just how far the art of filmmaking had come in twenty years, a revival of *The Great Train Robbery* had opened at the Astor.

There was so much to see, and unfortunately Garbo and Stiller had nothing better to do. There was no word from Schenck, or from Mayer on the West Coast. Stiller was furious. Obviously, the studio was stalling: what to do with this hotheaded director and the sullen, gangly actress? Someone in Dietz's office called her a "type"; but what *type* of type, no one could articulate: innocent? quiet? seductive? bookish? Disgusted more than discouraged, Garbo and Stiller considered cutting their losses and heading back to Stockholm. But then a Swedish friend turned their New York fortunes around. Martha Hedman, an actress and singer from Stockholm, and now one of Broadway producer David Belasco's star attractions, invited Garbo and Stiller into her intimate circle, an international bunch who made their fellow Europeans feel at home. One afternoon Hedman brought them around to meet Arnold Genthe, the German photographer. Eleanora Duse and Sarah Bernhardt had sat for Genthe, Anna Pavlova and Ellen Terry, too, and the teenaged Garbo suddenly spoke up, asking if he would make a photograph of her one day. In his memoirs, *I Remember New York,* Genthe says he was hoping she would make just such a request. "Why not now? You're here and I'm here and I must make some photographs of you to have visible proof that you are real." She protested, making excuses for her dress, her hair, her makeup. Genthe cut her off: "Never mind that. I am more interested in your eyes and in what is behind that extraordinary forehead." They worked for an hour in his studio, and Genthe was struck by the incredible variety in her face, later declaring that it was as if he had photographed several different women.

He showed the pictures to Frank Crowninshield, the editor of *Vanity Fair,* giving him "the opportunity to discover a great cinema star." Genthe also had one condition: The magazine must give the chosen photograph a full page. "A New Star from the North," filling page 80 of the November 1925 issue of *Vanity Fair,* introduces an amazingly worldly young woman, not yet twenty, delicately clutching at her throat, looking deliciously weary (in an actressy way) of life and love. It is a signature Genthe portrait —focus soft, lighting chiaroscuro, mood sensitive. Here is the future Garbo, not yet burnished, her pale mane brushed back from a slightly uneven hairline, eyebrows thick and natural. Her teeth, which needed straightening, do not show.

Genthe claims that it was his studies of Garbo that caused a current to run through Metro's dense executives: "Is that the blond Swede who has been hanging around here these last weeks," they exclaim in a boardroom scenario. "Great heavens!

If she can look like that we better sign her up. Don't let her get away!" But Genthe was writing after Garbo had become a star—Louis B. Mayer had already signed Garbo and Stiller in Europe, and by the time *Vanity Fair* hit the stands, they had at last crossed the United States, as ordered by Metro's Culver City headquarters. Before the end of the year Garbo was at work on *The Torrent*, which would capitalize on her glamour but also on her vulnerability and sophistication, qualities that come through in the Genthe portrait. The caption in *Vanity Fair* identifies her as the head-turner in *The Saga of Gösta Berling,* in which "she revealed such a fine dramatic instinct that many continental film companies bid high for her." That was not what had happened, but the Garbo legend was beginning. Stiller was not mentioned in the magazine.

Now that the wheels were in motion, perhaps Garbo began to question her relationship with Stiller, whose temper tantrums had caused her such anguish. She must not let Stiller interfere

*Sitting for Arnold Genthe, Garbo looked like no other nineteen-year-old on earth. Opposite: Vanity Fair's "New Star from the North."*

with her success, or even with her desire to act and make movies. "Right now I'm in a terrible hurry," she dashed off in a note dated August 30, 1925, to a Swedish friend on her last day in New York. "In a little while I'm off to California for the beginning of a long-term contract. My trunks are being carried out, which means that Greta also has to leave now! Don't forget me!" So she wrote from the Commodore Hotel, speaking of her future in the third person singular.

**M**an is always a spectator—we're spectators of our own lives. I've done it since I was born.

What you have in you is inborn; you don't learn it. But it does take someone to sit you down and tell you, to show you. Someone has to come along and open your horizons. If you're born in poverty and have nothing, absolutely nothing, and if nobody ever talks to you about anything, then you're a confined little thing.

You'll never get outside your narrow little margins— unless by some miracle somebody comes along and gets hold of you and puts you down on a bench and stands there in front of you, and shows you another way. Lots of things can happen to a child of fourteen who is very advanced.

Garbo was born into a family of severely limited means and she resolved early on to rise beyond her circumstances. As a neatly turned-out schoolgirl, her long hair cut in bangs, she performed well enough in class at Stockholm's Katarina Public School. But increasingly she dwelt in fantasies of life in the theater—she was determined to join a world, as she put it, "where a shepherdess could marry a king." Her rescue and enlightenment would arrive in the person of Mauritz Stiller, and their platonic story, of a star and her maker, truly is a twentieth-century take on Pygmalion and Galatea, or Svengali and Trilby.

She was an incredibly sensitive child, the third born to Anna Lovisa Karlsson and Karl Alfred Gustafsson, both from poor farming families. When Karl came of age he left the country to find a better life in Stockholm; Anna left for the city, too, hoping to find a man. Photographs of him reveal a strong Nordic countenance, and there is something aloof about him, too, a faraway look in his eyes. Anna seems an altogether different sort of person. Round and stout, with small, twinkling eyes and a sweet smile, she is a cookie-jar figure come to life. No marriage certificate has ever turned up, but Anna and Karl probably were wed the year they met, 1897. They soon had a son, Sven, and a daughter, Alva. On September 18, 1905, Greta Lovisa Gustafsson was born, like her brother and sister, in Stockholm's Southern Maternity Hospital. She came to be called "Kata," for the way she said her name as a little girl.

*Karl Alfred Gustafsson*

Though MGM would variously describe Garbo's father as a merchant, a grocer, and a small businessman (*Life* once referred to her as "the daughter of a machinist"), Karl Gustafsson probably was a butcher—a photograph shows him aproned, standing next to a side of beef. The family lived on Stockholm's South Side, in a bleak cityscape of gray brick tenements. The Gustafsson flat, four flights up a dark stairwell at 32 Blekingegatan, consisted of two rooms plus a cold-water kitchen. There was no toilet, only an outhouse behind the building. Such was the raw life of many in Sweden before the country's social-minded reforms took hold in the teens, a squalor that was almost Dickensian, especially in the winter, when families slept together to keep warm, and tuberculosis, "the disease of the poor," was rampant.

*Triumphant homecoming, 1928. Mother and daughter embrace.*

Anna—as her children called her—added to Karl's meager earnings by cleaning houses, riding buses to and from better neighborhoods than their own. "I'm sure she was a tough woman," says a longtime friend of Garbo's, who also grew up in Stockholm. "During that time, in that particular place, each day really was about survival. She was the one who kept the family together, and fed, and clean." By most accounts Kata was less industrious than her brother and sister, and apparently more indulged. A daydreamer, she carried on imaginary conversations with actors whose souvenir photographs she tore from magazines and pinned to the wall in her corner of the apartment. Karl encouraged her fantasies, walking her through Stockholm's theater district so that she could take in the marquees and, on the best days, get a glimpse of real-life actors. She became such a familiar presence at stage doors that custodians knew her by name and sometimes allowed her peeks inside. When Kata was seven years old, her father took her to Bromma Airport so that she could wave at Mary Pickford and Douglas Fairbanks, Hollywood royalty on a world tour.

> I used to go there at seven o'clock in the evening, when they would be coming in, and wait until eight-thirty, watching them ... listening to them get ready.... The big back door was always open even in the coldest weather.... Smell the greasepaint! There is no smell in the world like the backyard of a theatre. No smell will mean as much to me, ever.
>
> —GARBO, MARCH 1928

Karl Gustafsson was not as vigorous as he looked, and the brutality of his work affected his health. When he contracted tuberculosis, Greta abandoned her seventh-grade studies to nurse him and see him to a public clinic for treatments. His death came on June 1, 1920. "The same flesh, the same blood," she later recalled. "Yet he is gone . . . gone where you cannot see him, cannot talk to him."

A few weeks after her father's funeral, looking ample in her lacy confirmation dress, Greta took her first communion. She now was an adult in the eyes of the Lutheran Church, but she had always been so in her own. "I cannot remember being young, really young, like other children," she once told a reporter. (The sentiment turns up in an eerily autobiographical line in her final film, *Two-Faced Woman*, when she tells Melvyn Douglas, "I was born old.") One coming-of-age passage led to another, and by the end of the summer Greta decided not to return to school. She would go to work.

*P*eople need work. Sure there's dishwashing and sweeping alleys, but those jobs don't bring in any money. And they don't bring you any vistas, or put horizons in your head.

I was out today and saw a man standing with a little wagon, selling hot dogs and things, and he looked so sad. He looked so awful. He was pudgy, and you know probably he's twenty and he eats all his life only hot dogs, nothing else. He'll never know more, because he has no choice, he has no money. He has no way of finding out, nobody to tell him. All he has to do is push his cart out as early as possible to earn himself a living. How can the poor man learn? He has no *time,* and nobody ever talks to him about anything. I felt so sad for him: somebody's son being born and the mama says, "He'll probably be President one day." What for, what for? Presidents kill themselves too.

It's all chance, what you stumble onto.

In one of the opening scenes of *The Torrent,* her first Hollywood picture, Garbo comes upon her father as his barber is soaping his chin for a shave. The irony may not have been intended, though sly references to stars' lives and in-jokes were not uncommon on the silent screen. Garbo denied the stories, but it has often been said that at fourteen she worked as a *tvalflicka*—a "lather girl" in a barber shop. Her duties would have consisted of laying out towels and shaving gear, whipping up hot lather and brushing it into beards, and cleaning up afterward. The job required social skills, like a manicurist's today, and Greta was charming enough to earn some attractive tips on top of her meager wage.

Now with a little money of her own Greta at last was able to pay admission to a theater, and she bought herself a ticket to see Carl Brisson, a Danish prizefighter turned matinee idol who was appearing in a revue at the Mosebacke Theatre. Brisson later claimed to have lent a hand to Garbo's career, by receiving her in his dressing room, encouraging her to go into the theater, and arranging an introduction to the famous director Mauritz Stiller. But the only result of her night on the town was her resolve to

There is a young man in Sweden who proudly flaunts a bushy beard as a sign of his admiration for Greta Garbo.... [He] was her last customer before she sailed for Hollywood. When he learned she had departed, he swore that never would the hand of another maiden jab soap in his eye.... He ha[s] never shaved since."

—NEWSWIRE REPORT, 1930

find work that would get her closer to the world of the theater. Sales clerks were wanted at Bergstrom's, Stockholm's largest department store. Everyone important passed through Bergstrom's.

Perhaps Garbo owed her lifelong affection for B. Altman's, Saks, and other department stores to her pleasant tenure at Bergstrom's, where she was hired by the millinery department. She proved herself a dream salesgirl, crisp and chatty, and quick to show customers how to wear this or that *damhatt.* The store's managers featured her in the spring 1921 catalog, as five different *flickas:* "Clary" is the pouty one, "Ethel" almost haughty; "Helny" is a modest girl with downcast eyes, and "Solveig" is studious. Only as "Jane" does Greta smile.

A few months later she finally met the sort of customer she had hoped she would—Max Gumpel, an industrialist who took her to dinner and, apparently smitten, bought her jewelry. But then Greta was distracted by a motion-picture producer, Ragnar Ring, who arrived in her department to assemble a wardrobe for a promotional short he was making for the store. He also engaged her to play a comic bit in a sequence showing "How Not to Dress." In her brief performance she proves herself a good clown, thoroughly undone by an abundance of buttons, flaps, pockets, and scarves. In a second commercial, also to be shown in movie theaters, Greta advertises bakery products, by gobbling down cream puffs and cookies, and does so with amusing, plump-cheeked gusto. (Appearing in a cameo is Lars Hanson, who would star three times with Greta Garbo.)

After a year or so, Greta took a week's vacation at the country home of a friend from the store, and in a letter home revealed— at the age of sixteen—a hint of Garbo ennui, hypochondria, and misanthropy: "I have become rather indifferent to everything. This may be because I'm not in the best of health. I'm quite happy just being here and I don't miss Stockholm a bit. I wanted to come out to a place where there weren't many people and do nothing more than rest myself. I've been able to do that here. I spend almost all my time in my own company."

She returned to work in time to assist another producer in selecting costumes; and for an aspiring actress with a knack for comedy, Erik Petschler, known as the Mack Sennett of Sweden,

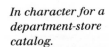

*In character for a department-store catalog.*

was the man to meet. Petschler liked Greta, baby fat and all, and cast her in his new movie, a bathing-beauty romp called *Peter the Tramp*. It was July of 1922, and Greta, who was not entitled to any more time off from the store, took another big step in her life: She quit her job. Before the end of the decade Bergstrom's was selling copies of her employee card, the bottom of which bears a space labeled "Reason for Leaving." In her bold script she gave her hopeful answer: "Left at own request to make a film."

Oh, *no* . . . the Salvation Army? They'll come to a Christmas Eve party? I never heard of such a thing. I think that's funny. That's probably the only way they can get money these days—people don't carry any money when they go out now, except for the taxi. Did they pass a tambourine? Did they get a drink for the hymns they sang—"Roll, Jordan, Roll" or whatever it is? I think that's sweet.

*Garbo clowns like a pro in her first whirl before a motion-picture camera.*

Some of the folklore of Garbo's early life has her exposed to live entertainment for the first time at a Salvation Army mission, where she eventually took to the stage herself, singing and dancing in benefits. (The 1990 edition of *Who's Who* says she began her career as a dancer, a goof that may have spun out of such tales.) It was not the Salvation Army, but Erik Petschler who provided Greta her next stepping-stone. After making his latest slapstick—in which Greta reveals her thick figure in a bathing suit, falls on her rump, sprinkles itching powder down a man's back, and swats him with a fish—Petschler boldly suggested that she apply for a government scholarship to the Academy of the Royal Dramatic Theater. The Academy, housed in the garret floors of the theater founded by King Gustavus III in 1788 was (and is) the essential training ground for actors in Sweden. Petschler introduced Greta to its retired director, the silver-haired eminence Frans Enwall, and his daughter, Signe, who would carry on the family's drama-coach tradition. Perhaps the Enwalls owed Petschler a favor, or perhaps they truly had seen potential in Greta's clowning on film; whatever transpired when they met, Signe volunteered to prepare the girl for her audition. If the jury of twenty-odd professionals and academics so ruled, Greta would be awarded a two-year scholarship to the Academy. She had only a few weeks to prepare for the annual auditions in August.

Fifty young hopefuls tried out, and the day seemed not to go well for Greta—the jury dismissed her before she had even finished her third reading, a monologue from Ibsen. But three days later the news arrived: She was one of six accepted. Classes would begin on September 18—her seventeenth birthday—and would include elocution, diction, posture, and movement. Greta would also study theater history and fencing, attend productions at the Royal Dramatic Theater, and occasionally take walk-on and small speaking parts. And Academy students would be tapped for local advertisements—indeed, Greta once posed behind the wheel of a Lancia roadster.

Feeling poorly educated and unsophisticated—a "South Sider"—Greta was at first extremely withdrawn and also a distracted student, "disgustingly late to class," in her words. But she soon began to feel comfortable among her fellow novices, who included Mona Martensen and Mimi Pollack, who would work in

Swedish and American films. The girls took to each other, staying up late to smoke cigarettes and talk about actors they admired. A class picture shows Greta, dressed all in black, at the far edge of a stylish group of twelve; she is looking not at the camera but at Pollack, and the two are holding hands.

Greta studied and played her assigned scenes, and the curriculum might suggest that the Academy typecast her, setting the mold for the future Garbo. In J. M. Barrie's light satire about household servants and their foolish masters, *The Admirable Crichton*, Greta played Fisher, a lady's maid described in the playwright's notes as "a superb creature . . . (who) often seems to be about to go to sleep in the middle of a remark . . . (and is) usually content to show that you merely tire her eyes." She took the lead in Victorien Sardou's Napoleonic romance *Madame Sans-Gêne*, as a beautiful laundress who does not tolerate loquaciousness, interrupting one character's rambling speech with an impatient "You chatter like a magpie!" In Ibsen's *The Lady from the Sea*, she was Ellida, who grows up in isolation and yearns for the sea. George Bernard Shaw described the character as "a helpless, idle . . . article of luxury." Greta's only Shakespeare suited her well: As Hermione, she poses as a statue in the fifth act of *The Winter's Tale;* gazing up at her, a lady of her court declares, "I like your silence, it the more shows off your wonder."

Questioned about Garbo today, Pollack nearly groans—she has been asked about her friend so many times this century. "Why such interest in Garbo for so many years?" she wonders, speaking slowly in English. "I cannot understand it." But she is cordial, this sole survivor of Garbo's Stockholm days, and she offers brief but fond words: "Greta was a lovely friend, and so fine an actress."

*I*t just takes that one person, an older someone who has lived life and seen things and made his way, to set you right. Then you can know yourself what's important and what to do.

*With classmates at the
Royal Academy. At far
right, an austere
Greta stands apart
with her friend Mimi
Pollack.*

All of the students at the Academy—indeed, many people in
Stockholm—were aware of Mauritz Stiller. Born in St. Petersburg,
Stiller, who was Jewish, fled the czar's military service in 1918
and made his way to Stockholm and the city's theater companies.
Although not particularly promising as an actor, Stiller possessed
fabulous gifts as a director. Drawn to the new medium of film, he
and Victor Sjöström brought Swedish cinema into its golden age
—Sjöström with *The Outlaw and His Wife* and *The Phantom Carriage,* Stiller with *Sir Arne's Treasure* and *Erotikon.* Stiller was an
imposing sight, tall and blond, with a long, rugged face and enormous features—he would have been a frightening presence had
he not been so flamboyant in his embroidered vests and floral-
patterned ties. He wore diamond stickpins in his lapels, and
showy rings on his fingers. Whizzing around Stockholm in his
canary-colored roadster, he was known as "the Yellow Peril," and
he loved the notoriety. Such a man would attract an eager entourage, but Stiller wanted only one disciple to embody his art, to be
his female alter ego.

In the winter of 1923, at the age of forty, he was preparing a new film and put out an audition call for a young actress, someone pliable and pretty. The Academy obliged him by sending over Mona Martensen and Greta Gustafsson. The exact sequence of events is now mired in the Garbo legend, but her first-person account of meeting Stiller was published in the April 1928 issue of *Photoplay:*

> One of the teachers came to me and said Mauritz Stiller wanted a girl to play in a picture for him. I said, "Ya? I will go and see him!" I didn't think much about it. I never get thrilled about anything until it happens. It hurts too much to be disappointed.
>
> That day, after school, I went up to his house to see him. . . .
>
> He was not at home, so I sat down and waited. Pretty soon he came in with his big dog. I started trembling all over.
>
> He seemed such a funny person. He looked at me, looked me up and down, looked me all over. He has told me since, exactly what I had on, even to my shoes and stockings.

*4 1*

*A man to fear, a maker of dreams: Mauritz Stiller in a rare quiet moment.*

At times it seemed as though he looked away, but I know he was really looking at me every moment....

Then he just looked at me some more and said, "What's your telephone number?" Then I knew it was all over.

Another version of the tale has Greta, increasingly astute and ambitious, taking the initiative before Stiller ever calls the Academy, setting out toward his office at the Swedish film company, Svensk Filmindustri, but getting lost along the way. She then turns up, unannounced, at his luxurious apartment. Twice rebuked by servants, she breaks the barrier on a third try and is led into the parlor, where, face to face with the man she knows can change her life, she haltingly recites a poem.

However she got there, invited or not, the fidgeting, unformed girl, too abashed even to remove her overcoat, haunted Stiller, who later said that he had "immediately noticed how easily one could dominate her by looking straight into her eyes." Before the week was out, Stiller had ordered a screen test. Greta admitted being "all shaky" when the day came around:

> I come off the street, go in and they make me up and then they take me in and tell me to lie in a bed and be sick. Very sick. I didn't know what it was all about. It seemed to me like a big joke, to come off the street and be right away sick. And I was ashamed....
>
> Stiller shouts, "My God, can't you be sick? Don't you know what it is to be sick? Great God!"
>
> Then I knew it wasn't play and it wasn't funny. I knew it was necessary in the movies and I became a very sick lady.

The star-is-born climax actually did occur in the way it has been told: Broken-winged, Greta hobbles home from the screen test and resigns herself to resuming her studies at the Academy. But two days later word arrives: She has won a starring role in Stiller's new film, *The Saga of Gösta Berling,* based on a beloved Swedish novel of the same title. She is to play a virtuous countess who is the salvation of a defrocked minister. The title role goes to Lars Hanson.

What in the world had Stiller seen in her? After the screen test he allegedly had turned to his crew and said, "You get a face like that before the camera once in a century." His infatuation with the girl baffled his colleagues. "None of us could understand why Stiller was so interested in this little nobody," said Stellan Clausson, the general production manager of Svensk Filmindustri. "To us, Greta appeared to be just an awkward, mediocre novice." But Stiller knew that his search was over—and he knew what he would call his discovery.

Greta Gustafsson did not inspire her new name, which Stiller apparently had concocted before he had ever seen her. Searching for a name that had a royal ring, but one that would sound the same in many languages, he began with the Hungarian "Gabor": Gabro, Gobra, Gorba . . . Garbo. That, anyway, is the enduring myth of the rechristening. He may actually have been inspired by Erica Darbo, a popular Swedish soprano of the day, and it also has been suggested that Greta herself created the name by combing a government registry and taking the prefix of one listing and the suffix of another.

A computerized search by international marketing experts couldn't come up with a more perfect name, for a star or a corporation or a building, than Garbo, two simple syllables of global resonance. Garbo, with a hard *g,* as in "great." A real word with Latin and Scandinavian roots, *garbo* means something like "grace" in its Spanish variation and describes a "wood nymph" in Norwegian. (The latter is what Louella Parsons must have been referring to when she reported that the name meant "a mysterious being who comes out in the night to dance in the moonlight.")

> I had it in my hands. Now I could get a little excited. The very best part in my very first picture.
> —GRETA GUSTAFSSON, 1923

A dramatization of the Gustafsson-to-Garbo metamorphosis made the rounds in the wake of her fame, in a scenario that has Stiller saying to her, "Your name, it is bad . . . too long for theaters and pictures, too difficult for foreigners to pronounce. Now I have thought of two from which you may choose. The first is Greta Garbo. That is easy to say.... The other I also like. It is Gussie Berger." With that, Stiller gives her until the next morning to decide, but she had already made up her mind: "I will be Greta Garbo." (If the episode is true, it likely is the origin of Garbo's sometime alias, Gussie Berger.)

Application for the change of name was made to the Swedish Registry, and on November 9, 1923, Anna Gustafsson signed the necessary documents for her underage daughter.

*I* 'll tell you a little secret, for all it's worth: If you get your figure trimmed down just once, it's not so difficult to keep it. But you have to get trim first. That first time is what's important. By experience I can tell you that. Someone told me that once.

Stiller now set out to remake the creature he likened to "wax in my hands." The first thing he sought to do was to streamline her figure. "With your broad shoulders, narrow hips, and sleek head, you can take on the glamour of the Egyptian beauties of old," he told her, according to a colorful account of the day. "But first you must get slim. Slim as a match." Stiller took over her life, telling her what to eat, teaching her how to dress, showing her the proper way to stand, to recline, to walk across a room. Dieting and spending hours in a Stockholm sauna, Garbo grew slim—alarmingly so to some. "Her breasts don't show anymore," Mimi Pollack wrote to a friend. "They've become like two buttons." From her office window at Svensk Filmindustri, Stellan Clausson watched Stiller and Garbo pace for hours in a wooded grove behind the studio. "Stiller was always preaching, Greta solemnly listening and learning," she said. "I never saw anyone more earnest." What a pair they must have made in Stockholm, the flashy Stiller calling for the meek Garbo at the palatial Academy, then dropping her off at her tenement. It is not known whether he ever met her family, or if Anna Gustafsson had reservations about her daughter's constant and much older companion. As they would in Hollywood, people in Stockholm whispered that Garbo and

As she wrote it all her life, Garbo's signature was broad and uncomplicated, the large, loopy letters not a bit cryptic, nor the mark of someone particularly delicate or temperamental. In her personal correspondence, she would lightly scratch her name or her initials—the double *G* —in pencil.

Stiller were lovers; their friends, though, understood that his passion for women was an idealized kind.

Stiller was merciless with Garbo during the making of *The Saga of Gösta Berling*. "But wait," he is reported to have said to his crew. "When I'm through with her she'll please the very gods." Like an obsessed lover, he seemed never to take his eyes off Garbo, scrutinizing and criticizing her every blink and movement, sometimes in a terrible show of temper. "He told me to practice alone," she recalled. "But I knew he was in some corner. . . . I looked all around and could not see him, but I knew he was there."

She cried some days, and once cursed him in front of the cast and crew. But she forgave him and denied rumors of their difficulties. "Stiller is the most generous person I know," she told a Swedish journalist who visited the set. "One never gets angry or sad, however much he rebukes one. He creates people and shapes them according to his will." Her trust in him was like bedrock, her devotion and obedience complete. "I would say, 'Is it good?' And he would say, 'It is good.' And so I would do it."

Running nearly four hours in length, the lavish *Saga of Gösta Berling* opened in Stockholm in the spring of 1924, at the time the most expensive film made in Sweden. Audiences cheered—particularly during a climactic chase across an icy plain, wolves nipping at the heroine's sleigh—but critics did not, chiefly because Stiller had taken such liberties in giving the novel a happy ending. (The novelist, Selma Lagerlöf, the first woman awarded the Nobel Prize for literature, was displeased with the film and said so in print.) Scandinavian reviews were mixed but no one called it Stiller's finest, nor had much to say about the girl who played the precociously womanly yet virginal Countess Elisabeth Dohna.

But in Germany the film was considered brilliant. For the premiere stars and director were brought to Berlin and Garbo, wrapped in fur and ensconced at the Esplanade Hotel, experienced a heady few weeks. She liked the Germans for their way of showing affection *aus der ferne* (from the distance), later observing, "The German people are wonderful—they do not touch you, yet they have their arms around you, always."

*The Saga of Gösta Berling* proved to be tremendously popular throughout the Continent, and its distributors, the Trianon Com-

After Garbo's move
Hollywood, her
brother and sister
took her new name
for their own acting
careers, such as the
were. Alva, sadly, d
not live long, but
apparently had mu
promise—Garbo
herself said that Al
was a wonderful
actress and a beaut
far greater than sh
Sven Garbo acted
briefly in France ar
then, reclaiming th
name Gustafsson,
took up painting.

pany, gave Stiller a starter budget of a million marks for his next production. Determined to put Garbo in an exotic setting, he concocted a Crimean War drama about a convent girl who winds up in a Turkish harem—Garbo of course would play the imperiled one. With a fabulous expense account, Stiller booked passage on the Orient Express for his cast. In Constantinople they got as far as scouting locations—a treat for Garbo, who was fascinated by the sights and smells of the ancient city—when the news arrived that the entire project had collapsed: Trianon had gone bankrupt. Stiller preceded Garbo back to Berlin, leaving her to pursue the kind of solitary and peripatetic pleasures she would enjoy in New York City in the 1980s. "I walked around, by myself mostly . . . but I was not lonely," she said of her time alone in Constantinople. "One day I was following along behind one of the old Turks—a dirty one with funny pants . . . I do not know how many hours I followed him. He did not go anywhere, did not have anywhere to go but wander. I liked it."

Back in Berlin, Garbo seemed philosophical about the fiasco, or at most unconcerned. "Don't worry," she wrote to her mother. "Everything will be all right. The beginning was good, in any case." She was not idle for long. G. W. Pabst, the German director, approached Garbo about a lead role in *Joyless Street*, a grim portrait of society's moral corruption in postwar Vienna. Greta was eager to continue working, and Stiller, needing money, negotiated well for her, securing a fee of $4,000 paid in United States currency. Without Stiller behind the camera Garbo was jumpy, but Pabst was patient with her. Though Stiller drilled her on scenes at night back at their hotel and sometimes butted in on the set, Garbo must have begun to realize that there were other filmmakers who could draw fine things from her.

Some who have seen the ten-reel original say that *Joyless Street* is a masterpiece comparable to the director's *Threepenny Opera* and *Pandora's Box*. As it was released, cut first by censors and then by commercial distributors for length, it is a beautiful shadowed thing to look at, but the story is nearly impossible to follow. Pabst got a strong performance from Garbo as Greta Rumfort, the daughter of a respectable family who is forced into prostitution by hunger and a greedy landlord—and he meant it as a compliment when he balked at her suggestion that they work

*Garbo was all innocence and sweet virtue as the Countess Elisabeth Dohna in* The Saga of Gösta Berling.

Her meanderings through Turkish bazaars afforded one of Garbo's most passionate admirers, the noble-nosed poet Mercedes de Acosta, a first glimpse of her future friend—and, in her memoir, *Here Lies the Heart,* the chance to sound as lovesick as Aschenbach trailing Tadzio:

"One day in the lobby of the Pera Palace Hotel I saw one of the most hauntingly beautiful women.... Her features and her movements were so distinguished and aristocratic looking that I decided she must be a refugee Russian princess....

"Several times after this I saw her in the street. I was terribly troubled by her eyes and I longed to speak to her, but I did not have the courage.... I did not even know what language to use. She gave me the impression of great loneliness.... I hated to leave without speaking to her, but sometimes destiny is kinder than we think, or maybe it is just that we cannot escape our destiny. Strangely enough ... I had a strong premonition that I might again see [that] face on some other shore."

Two years later de Acosta received a letter from her friend, the photographer Arnold Genthe, who enclosed a portrait of his latest subject, a young Swede on her way to Hollywood. A gasp as she opened the envelope: "There before me," she wrote, "was the beguiling face of the haunting person I had seen in Constantinople."

Garbo would later refer to de Acosta as "that crazy mystic Spaniard."

*In her second feature film, G. W. Pabst's* Joyless Street, *Garbo mastered the art of suffering.*

together again, telling her that any future collaboration would be considered a Garbo film, not a Pabst film.

*A*nyone who has a continuous smile on his face conceals a toughness that is almost frightening.

In November of 1924 Louis B. Mayer arrived in Berlin by way of Rome (where he had rushed to check cost overruns on his $6 million production of *Ben-Hur*). The mogul of course knew of Stiller, and had been encouraged to hire him by Victor Sjöström, who, as Victor Seastrom, was already successfully making his way at Metro as a writer, director, and actor. Mayer was especially keen on Stiller after seeing the European box-office receipts for *The Saga of Gösta Berling,* which was just the sort of prestige hit he wanted for the studio. A meeting was arranged at the Adlon

Hotel, where the Mayers were staying. Traveling with him were his wife, Maggie, and their daughters, Edith and Irene.

In her memoirs, Irene Mayer Selznick describes her father's reaction to the Stiller film as they sat in a Berlin projection room: "The only advance reservation my father had [about hiring Stiller] was the stipulation that he wouldn't come without [Garbo], an obstacle my father thought he could overcome. In-

A decade after her work with Pabst, when David O. Selznick was working with Garbo to keep her career on its elegant track, *Joyless Street* came round in a way that might have haunted her. A film distributor named Samuel Cummins had imported a few random reels of it and, as Selznick wrote to Nicholas Schenck, planned to cash in on it "as a burlesque," something that could embarrass Metro's top star. The lack of further correspondence on the matter suggests it was resolved; but Selznick was again alarmed when producers at Time Inc. asked if Metro would provide early photographs and Swedish film footage for a "March of Time" newsreel about Garbo's rise to the top. Selznick did not like the idea "of . . . Garbo looking grotesque . . . which can do nothing but lower her audience value." But *Time*'s Henry Luce wanted to tell the whole rags-to-riches story, from the unrefined Greta Gustafsson to the goddess Garbo. "Can readily understand your company's reaction to Garbo matter," Luce wired Selznick. "[But] original idea was humanly interesting success story . . . showing able young shopgirl's arrival at top and repeated triumphs there. Net effect anything but laughs at her expense. Surely best biographies are those where character starts humbly and ends high. Surely soundest screen popularity not based on remote idolatry." MGM's response is not known, but it must have been a persuasive statement of the studio's position, for the newsreel showing the star's homely years never was made.

stead, Miss Garbo overcame him in the first reel. . . . Dad said, 'I'll take Stiller all right. As for the girl, I want her even more . . . I can make a star out of her. I'll take them both.' "

If that is true, then Mayer's indifference toward Garbo when they met for dinner is hard to understand. Though Stiller had dressed and placed Garbo just so, Mayer smiled benignly in her direction but said nothing to her. Conversing in German, or Yiddish, the men struck a deal, and Stiller didn't have to fight for his steep terms: Mayer agreed to pay him $1,500 per week, and didn't balk when he said he wouldn't come without Garbo. Fine—she would start at $350. Contracts would be drafted at once and sent to them back in Stockholm for signature. As some accounts have it, the strongest evidence that Mayer had been aware of Garbo's presence was in his brusque parting words to Stiller: "Tell her to lose some weight. American men don't like fat girls." If Mayer, still smiling, meant to intimidate Garbo, he probably did. But as he would learn, their first business meeting did not set a pattern for those to come.

Anna Gustafsson would again act on behalf of her underage daughter, co-signing the MGM contract. Greta left the Academy, but even as she and Stiller were being congratulated they were having second thoughts: Why leave home for Hollywood? They were the most talked-about team in European film—dare they risk their art and their relationship? And Greta's sister was not well—how could she leave now? But her mother encouraged her independence, saying, "I think you know better. I want you to go where you should." As the day of departure approached, though, Stiller wired Mayer in Culver City: Could they be released from the contract? Came the sharp reply of June 20, 1925: "Get on the next boat."

And so they went, by ship and by rail, halfway around the world, settling seaside, in Santa Monica, in Hollywood's Scandinavian colony. Victor Seastrom was there with his Finnish wife, Evastoff Seastrom, and Lars Hanson, a new MGM import himself, with his wife, Karin Molander; also the actors Einar Jansen, who had worked with Garbo in the Pabst film, Sven Gade, Karl Dane, and Ben Christiansen, and the designer Erik Stocklossa. They all adored Garbo. It was a beautiful spot, and isolated—about as far as one could get from Culver City and still be within commuting

*With a fellow
Swede in Hollywood,
the director Victor
Seastrom.*

distance to the studio. But Garbo ached for home, almost instantly, and she worried, as she had in New York, that she and Stiller had no assignment. Why had Mayer rushed them? If she had moments of happiness during her first few weeks in California, they came with Stiller in his lighter moments, and with herself, alone on the beach, walking in her bare feet along the water's edge. As she wrote to Vera Schmiterlov, a friend from the Academy: "I live in a very lonely place where I am left absolutely alone, go out for walks [and] look at the sky and the water and speak to myself."

Garbo had always loved the ocean, but her spirits on this coast were anything but pacific.

*L*ife is full of melancholy times. These things come, but luckily they go away . . . otherwise we'd jump in the East

River, and it's so filthy. Some people, they go over a rooftop, that's how bad they have it. Even a teenaged girl who's very advanced can feel she can't cope with life and commits suicide. There are all kinds of human beings in this world and they're down in such depths you can't even imagine it, the unfathomable depths. It's incredible what goes on inside human beings.

Luckily we didn't get that bad. You're too young to be in such an emotional state. Yet, yet . . . things will come later on that can strike you down. Life goes on and things happen: Come along with me and you'll see differently. My dear young man, if it were just a question of simple frustration . . . it's not just that, it's the human condition, it's the human situation. Well, we mustn't wade in this today, kid.

**3 THE STAR**

Preceding page: *A pensive moment on the set of her first comedy, and her next-to-last film,* Ninotchka.

*I* wish one were living in a perfect climate, where you'd never have to leave if you didn't want to. A place with a perfect climate, whatever a perfect climate is. What's a perfect climate? Southern California? Or is that too perfect?

Try to figure out where you've been the happiest. I'm still attached to California, because I was there for so long. I will never get out of that feeling. But you have to leave Hollywood. I knew a German movie director who left, too —Murnau—who came over to work in America. He worked in Hollywood, but he didn't like it very much. They sent him to Tahiti. He came back and sold whatever he had and said, "I'm going there and I'm never coming back." But before he could leave Hollywood he was killed in an automobile accident.*

All those years—I'll always have strong feelings about California.

---

* F. W. (Friedrich Wilhelm) Murnau, the German director of *Nosferatu* and *The Last Laugh*, made three films for Fox, including the landmark *Sunrise*. After shooting *Tabu* in Tahiti, Murnau intended to move there, in the so-long-to-civilization spirit of Gauguin. Some notoriety accompanied his death, at the age of forty-two, in 1931: It was said that he and his Filipino companion were in flagrante delicto when Murnau's Packard hit a post and tumbled over an embankment. It was enough of a scandal that few in the Hollywood community would risk attending his funeral. Garbo did. She admired Murnau and had hoped to work with him. It was said that she commissioned a death mask of Murnau, though it did not appear among her estate possessions.

Garbo's fondness for California was not immediate, and she was not made to feel particularly welcome when she first set foot there. A blurry photograph of her and Mauritz Stiller, taken on the train platform at Pasadena's Southern Pacific Station on a September afternoon in 1925, accompanied "The Foreign Legion in Hollywood," *Photoplay*'s tirade against the "invaders who are pouring in with the American motion picture industry as their objective and American dollars as their goal." Ignoring the fact that the industry was founded and run by immigrants, the unsigned piece actually used the word "menace" to describe the likes of Mauritz Stiller, Pola Negri, Ernst Lubitsch, Emil Jannings, Erich Pommer, and Erich von Stroheim. "The foreigners are going through the studios with the speed of mumps through a day

*A frizzy-haired hopeful—Stiller looming behind her—arrives in Hollywood.*

*Posing with MGM's Leo the Lion in one of the studio's early publicity pictures.*

nursery," the piece went. "Every lot is swollen with them. They're not all stars. There are foreign cameramen, directors, scenarists, dress designers, too, and they all bring a relative along."

Irene Mayer Selznick recalled that Garbo "began as a star" at the studio, that she did not have to come up through the ranks, as Joan Crawford and Norma Shearer had. It is true that Garbo was never a chorus girl, or even a supporting player; but before her debut in *The Torrent* she was subjected to the standard humiliations of starlet publicity. It was as if no one at Metro had seen the *Vanity Fair* photograph, revealing the young woman's mature eroticism and cosmopolitan cool. For its first batch of publicity pictures, the studio teamed its new "Swedish pastry" with track stars at the University of Southern California. The results were awful: Garbo as mascot, her chest making no impression on a skimpy USC T-shirt; Garbo "on your mark"; Garbo nervously standing under the high-jump bar as a lanky boy sails overhead; Garbo in a crouch, hurdled by jocks.

Next stop was Gay's Lion Farm, where the aspiring actress was seated next to the real-life model for the MGM logo. As much as she truly loved animals, Garbo—in a fur-trimmed leather coat —is not relaxed with this one, and she shows it, leaning as far from the beast as she can and still stay within the frame of the picture. "That poor girl was almost paralyzed with fear," the photographer, Don Gillum, later admitted. "Suddenly she made a beeline for the restroom and I had to drag her out. . . . She had to be thrust into the cage." Over the next few weeks, the studio sent out more photographs of Garbo: strumming a ukelele, chatting with an Indian prince, smelling a carnation.

Why did she agree to such posing? Why did Stiller allow it? Probably they were powerless to object—the studio's usual procedure was to reserve the right to use a player's name and image in whatever way it deemed advantageous. Besides, Garbo was wise to appear cooperative, especially after Stiller's tantrums in New York. She cared deeply about her career. She wanted success. On Metro's routine publicity department questionnaire, after "Goals and Ambitions," she'd written, "To be a great star"; *Movie Mirror* quoted her as saying, "I like my work. I want to be a big actress. That is natural. Do you not want to be big in what you are doing?"

Ruth Harriet Louise's portraits, made in the 1920s, were an exception to the studio's uninspired early publicity photographs of Garbo. Exactly the star's age, Louise captured an unaffected, even girlish Garbo (much unlike the woeful woman in the Arnold Genthe studies). For Louise, Garbo actually smiled, and appeared more casual—unmasked—than she ever would for Clarence Bull or in her one sitting with George Hurrell. Louise's work with Garbo is all the more remarkable because she never photographed her in close-up, but at the distance required to get the full figure. In Louise's portraits, Garbo seems confidently herself; in one she is wearing men's white pajamas—bottom cuffs rolled up, top open above a snowy cleavage—and she is barefoot. Louise arrived at Metro the same year that Garbo did, 1925, and though she quickly distinguished herself among her male peers, she left the studio rather mysteriously—Garbo-like—in 1930. She died in 1944, and may have been saved from obscurity in the winter of 1991, when *Premiere Magazine* included a tribute to her in its special edition, "100 Years of Moviemaking."

Opposite: *Garbo photographed by Ruth Harriet Louise.*

**C**alifornia can be a marvelous place to get things done, to work. Marvelous, really. The sun is always there, and the days are long. You think the sun will never go down. People go for hours there, up early, out late, going like mad, even if they don't know what they're doing.

Garbo and Stiller diligently reported to Culver City, he to angle for directing assignments, she to wait for one to come through. Both were struck by how differently things were done in the American film industry. In Europe, they were accustomed to shooting on location and working for months on a picture; here, the process happened so rapidly, and on strict shooting schedules

of twenty to thirty days. "You make any climate you want, right in the studio," Garbo marveled. "You finish a picture in a few weeks. I don't know whether I like it or not."

Lillian Gish, an established star but new on the Metro lot, was making *The Wind*, and her set became Garbo's idling ground. "Anyone could come and watch that wanted to," said Gish. "It didn't bother me. . . . You couldn't let anything bother you while the camera was going. . . . Mr. Stiller would put her on our set in the morning, and come to get her at noontime, take her to lunch, then put her back there." A photograph exists of the two women —Gish in costume, holding a broom, Garbo with a scarf over her head—and it seems that they are sharing a confidence.

Their friendship would be sealed a half-year later, when Garbo, during the filming of *The Temptress*, received news from home that her sister, Alva, had died of tuberculosis. As Gish recalled the day: "I thought, 'My goodness, how would I feel if I were in a strange country and didn't have money and couldn't go if my sister died?' . . . She couldn't speak English, and I couldn't speak Swedish to tell her I was sorry. So I sent her some flowers, with a note. She came up to me and tried to thank me, burst into tears, and so did I."

Lillian Gish—Garbo's first friendly American—may also be the person most responsible for getting the gears turning for the young Swede, by encouraging her ace, soft-focus cameraman, Hendrik Sartov, to take some close-up shots of her. Stiller worked with Sartov on what became the only thing resembling a screen test Garbo ever got at MGM. One version has Mayer and Thalberg overwhelmed by the test, but only after Gish (or Stiller, or Victor Seastrom) forces them to look at it. In a richer telling, the footage is forgotten until director Monta Bell comes upon it in a reel of stock flood scenes he is perusing for *The Torrent*. Between frames of bursting dams—eureka: Bell has found his leading lady.

Along the way, Gish would also help Garbo less directly, setting an example with the demands she made on studio executives and with the decorum she brought to her career. Like Lon Chaney, Gish shunned promotional gimmickry. When Garbo declared her own moratorium, she was mimicked around town: "I vill be glad when I am a beeg star like Miss Geesh. Then I vill not need publicity and have peectures taken with prize fights."

It was a blow to Stiller not to be chosen to direct Garbo in her first film for Metro, but since it was the only project offered her, he advised her to proceed. He would be her de facto director, anyway, drilling her every evening, sometimes late into the night. *The Torrent* had attractive commercial possibilities: It was based on a story by the popular Spanish novelist Vicente Blasco Ibáñez, whose *Four Horsemen of the Apocalypse* had inspired the 1921 superstar-making vehicle for Rudolph Valentino. Though liberal sentiments otherwise fill his work, Blasco Ibáñez was no feminist, and Leonora Moreno of *The Torrent* was typical of his cutout female characters, nice girls ruined by lust and ambition. Garbo's Leonora was a sweet-voiced peasant who, rejected by her lover, becomes the jaded diva known as "La Brunna" (loosely, the Dark One). In Dorothy Farnum's script notes, La Brunna is several sizes larger than life: "an unconventional diva, an extraordinary personality, an abnormal being . . . a woman with a healthy appetite—for life and for food! The story's unique twist, according to conference notes, is that "it argues against respectability." The script plays as badly as it reads on the page, and the costumes look like Halloween; but Garbo, lit by William Daniels, prevails.

61

*For her MGM debut, Garbo was portrayed as a raven-haired vamp.*

This was her first collaboration with Daniels, who saw that Garbo was better photographed in close-up and long shots, nothing in between. He would serve as chief cameraman on all but six of her twenty-four Metro films.

When she first appears on the American screen, Garbo is praying, a *señorita* on her knees. "Leonora's prayers were simple," runs the subtitle. "That Don Rafael Brull would that day pass her way. That the voice which God had given her might bring wealth and ease to her parents." She then rises to sing (to a little bird) and mouth her first words (to her father): "Dona Bernarda has called about the mortgage money." Then (to her father's barber): "Will you carry a note to Don Rafael?" The performance, as seen in daily rushes, was sufficient to convince the studio to build the movie's promotion around Garbo (and, of course, the special-effects torrent):

> Ibanez' *Torrent!* Rushing flood of mighty emotion!
> Sweeping us on—ever on—breathless . . .
> Greta Garbo—perfection!
> Discovered by Metro-Goldwyn-Mayer in stark Sweden!
> She is setting the heart of America aflame!

The picture opened on Washington's Birthday, 1926, and *Variety* predicted a hit and a star: "Greta Garbo . . . might just as well be hailed right here as the find of the year. This girl has everything with looks, acting ability and personality. When one is a Scandinavian and can put over a Latin characterization with sufficient power to make it most convincing, need there be any more said? . . . Louis Mayer can hand himself a few pats on the back for having brought [her] over from the other side." Garbo's arrival, added the *New York Telegram,* "justified the precedent ballyhoo," and Hearst's *American* welcomed the "young, slim [actress], with strange, haunting eyes. . . . She proves that the murmurs of praise which heralded her appearance were too feeble by far." Virtually the only dissent came from the *Evening Graphic* (which, half a year earlier, had published the photograph of Garbo and Stiller disembarking in New York): "No doubt in some roles, Greta may be an addition to the list of feminine film favorites, but neither her type nor her acting is of the vivid quality to impress us."

Garbo and Stiller agreed with the minority opinion—they

63

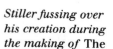

*Stiller fussing over his creation during the making of* The Temptress.

hated her performance and the picture, and Stiller was determined to show what magic they could make as a team, now that he was assigned to her next. But on the set of *The Temptress,* another Blasco Ibáñez potboiler, Stiller caused chaos from the first, and episodes from his brief tenure sound comic: the director taking up the megaphone to shout (in Swedish or German or nonsensical English) at people standing a few feet away; calling in scores of extras and not using them; banishing everyone, including executives, from the set; ordering Antonio Moreno, as feisty as Latin lovers come, to shave off his silly moustache. But Stiller lavished attention on Garbo, and a photograph from the production catches him as mad maestro, coaxing impossible perfection from his prodigy.

Worse than displaying bad behavior, Stiller went recklessly over budget—in fact, he didn't seem to realize that films *had* such things as budgets. He didn't last two weeks, and before firing him, an incredulous Irving Thalberg is said to have shouted, "Is this man mad? Has he ever been behind a camera before?" Fred Niblo, a handyman among Metro's stable of directors (valued for his economical handling of such films as *The Mark of Zorro* and *The Three Musketeers*), was called in to finish the film. "This new director they gave us is always asking me if I'm *happy*," Garbo

*THE STAR*

Later in Garbo's career, MGM's press department made much of her bewildering early months in California (by way of apologizing for her uncooperative way with the press):

*Every night as she journeyed toward the ocean from the studio, she wondered how she could force herself to return the next morning. She wanted to run away. To pack her bags and return to the friendly faces she knew and longed for. . . . The strange faces surrounding her were frightening. The humor was strange; she couldn't understand the source of laughter. It was only natural that, in the back of her mind, would flash the thought that perhaps they were laughing at her. Then and there was born the desire to shut herself away from prying eyes, not because of temperament, but rather because of terror.*

wrote home. "You know, these Americans don't understand us Europeans." But she played on, as Elena, the naughty marquise of *The Temptress,* returning to Santa Monica each evening to nurse Stiller's ego and his worrisome rheumatism. She spoke out in his defense, saying, "Mr. Stiller is an artist, he does not understand about the American factories. . . . In our country it is always the small studio. He does not understand the American business." Also grieving for her sister, who died shortly after Stiller had been fired, Garbo described herself as "broken to pieces . . . so tired I [don't] know what to do."

Stiller's extravagant contributions to *The Temptress* survive in its opening banquet scene, fraught with sexual intrigue, followed by an elaborately choreographed masked ball. Though Garbo could hardly bear to look at the rest of the film, it was a second triumph for her. Mordaunt Hall of the *New York Times* praised her "minimum of gestures and an unusual restraint in her expressions." Robert E. Sherwood crumbled in the humor magazine *Life:* "I want to go on record as saying that Greta Garbo in *The Temptress* knocked me for a loop. I had seen [her] once before, in *The Torrent,* and had been mildly impressed by her visual effectiveness. [Now] this effectiveness proves to be positively devastating."

Thanks to Erich Pommer's influence, Stiller landed a contract at Paramount, and at a thousand dollars more per week than Metro paid him. It was almost unthinkable to him that he and Garbo had been torn apart, that he was now working for a rival studio, directing Pola Negri in *Hotel Imperial.* But his career was on the line, and in a virtually sleepless, month-long frenzy (probably with a translator on hand), Stiller delivered the film on time and under budget. The picture was a success, if not a sensation; but if Thalberg had second thoughts about having fired Stiller, they vanished with the director's next two, a Negri vehicle called *The Woman on Trial,* and *The Street of Sin,* starring Fay Wray and Emil Jannings. Stiller's contrariness resurfaced; and when neither picture found an audience, Paramount dropped him. Appealing to MGM, he asked for one more chance to direct Garbo—now with four Metro films behind her—as Sarah Bernhardt in *The Divine Woman.* Victor Seastrom got the job, and Stiller packed up for Sweden.

It is hard to know what Garbo was feeling at this development. For personal reasons, she was undoubtedly sad to see Stiller go, and sorry about his difficulties and failures. She cried when she saw him off at Southern Pacific Station, and probably meant it when she told him she would join him soon; after all, Lars Hanson had already returned to Sweden, in triumph, to resume his acting career there, and she had planned to do the same. But professionally, Garbo must have been relieved, or at least

It has been suggested that Metro was relieved to see Stiller go, not just because of the professional anguish he caused the studio but because of the potential embarrassment that could come with revelations about his private life. Whether Stiller suffered discrimination and intimidation because of his sexuality probably will never be known.

ambivalent, about Stiller's departure, after the problems he had caused her in Berlin, in New York, and now in California. After all, if she truly hadn't wanted him to go, she could have intervened: Garbo was now in a position to get Stiller a job, if not on *The Divine Woman,* then on some other Metro picture. Apparently, she chose not to.

Eight months had passed when, on the morning of November 8, 1928, Garbo was interrupted on the jungle-camp set of *Wild Orchids.* She was standing by, waiting to play a scene with Nils Asther. A telegram had arrived from Stockholm: Stiller was dead. Emmanuel Sarnoff was the nineteen-year-old office boy who delivered the wire, and he contradicts all published accounts of the drama, which have Garbo turning ashen and walking off the set to compose herself. Sarnoff says that Garbo remained standing as she read, then suddenly sat down and "started to look sad." A string trio that had been playing background music suddenly was silent. Wanting to linger, Sarnoff wandered over to a partition, tried nonchalantly to lean on it—and fell through, collapsing a wall of South Seas scenery. It was real-life comic relief, as everyone—including Garbo, with tears in her eyes—roared with laughter. Later that day she asked to be released from the picture, warning Louis B. Mayer that she "would be dead on the screen." He was not sympathetic, however, and Garbo finished the film. Then she was off for Sweden, defying orders to start work on *The Single Standard.* A trip home was long overdue; it was time to see her family—and to visit the graves of her sister and Stiller.

It has been claimed that Stiller died while clutching one of the Arnold Genthe photographs of his ideal beloved, and considering the hugeness of the man's passions and his sense of drama, perhaps those indeed were the particulars of his death

> My poor body wasn't able to carry on any longer. I was so tired, so sick, so heartbroken.... I am not the kind of girl who can powder my nose and say, "Ah, go on with you."
>
> GARBO, NOVEMBER 1928

scene. It is not true that he died of elephantiasis—a rumor inspired by the size of his features. Rather, the rheumatic fever he had been suffering seems to have finally affected his heart. And though Stiller had plunged back into work in Sweden, it is fair to say that his spirit, even his will to live, had been broken in Hollywood.

On the voyage over Garbo was invited to join a royal party on board, headed by Sweden's young Prince Sigvard. His friend Wilhelm Sorensen was along, as well as the Count and Countess of Wachmeister, and they were all eager to meet the former salesgirl from Stockholm's South Side. The turn of fortune was not lost on Garbo, who reportedly said of her aristocratic admirers, "They wouldn't have wanted to know me back in Sweden—why should I want to know them now?"

> Garbo actually cherished her homeland's throne, and in 1983, quite proudly accepted its highest civilian decoration. By order of King Carl XVI Gustaf, she was made a Commander of the Swedish Order of the North Star. Count Wilhelm Wachmeister did the honors in a small private ceremony in the East End Avenue apartment of Jane Gunther.
>
> She apparently felt differently toward Britain's royal family, some of whom had been scrambling for an introduction for decades. "Once they get the smell of greasepaint in their nostrils," she told a friend in the mid-1970s, "they won't let you go."

Garbo extended her 1929 homecoming by months and Mayer grew livid about his truant star. But the reviews of *Wild Orchids* reminded him of her worth. "It is really not such a long time since the American screen knew not Greta Garbo," said the *Mid-Week Pictorial*. "But already it has become rather difficult to recall how it felt to live in that benighted period." The *Detroit Free Press* ended its rave with the hope that Garbo "will come back from Sweden and give America more."

*T*here's nothing to laugh at today—there's the income tax instead. I like to be close to the bank—do you? It shouldn't be too far, because you never know when you'll need what you have there. It shouldn't be a terribly far walk to get there. Don't you think all banks take a little bit from us? Steal? I'm sure they do, but I never check my bank statements. I think I should, but it's all too much for me, even with a calculator. What would I do with an adding machine anyway—what'll I add? The minute I see numbers and figures I go cross-eyed.

The truth is that Garbo had a terrific head for dollars and cents, and her bank balance must have set some sort of record for a woman who worked for only fifteen years of a long life. Though she was among those who lost heavily in the 1929 bank collapse, she recovered almost immediately from the panic and by 1933 was the highest-paid woman in Hollywood, perhaps in the country, earning $250,000 per film. Listing her among the ten richest women in Hollywood, Hedda Hopper quipped that Garbo "has more than half of the first nickel she ever earned. . . . She's got it—all of it."

Garbo probably deserved her reputation for being stingy, and years after she left Hollywood she confided to her friend Eleanor Lambert that the trait stemmed from the traumatic events of her past. Says Lambert, "She told me that after her father had died in humiliating circumstances, with no dignity or privacy, she made a promise to herself then, at that young age, that she would never be poor again." And so over the years Garbo invested wisely, chiefly on the advice of two men, Gayelord Hauser, with whom she bought up blue-chip commercial property on Rodeo Drive (they were landlords to such tenants as Gucci and Hermes), and George Schlee, who guided many of her purchases of art, antiques, and company stock. Apart from her contributions to war relief, Garbo hoarded her funds, making virtually no charitable gestures, not even posthumously. In her will, Garbo assigned her entire estate to her closest living relative, her niece, Gray Gustafsson Reisfield (whose father, Sven Gustafsson, died in 1941). Clare Kroger, her Swiss housekeeper of thirty years, received what she will only describe as "two small paintings," and a few months' pension. But, she adds, "I'm satisfied. She was a very sweet lady."

In California Garbo lived frugally, famously so—she was as tight-fisted as Jack Benny pretended to be, though no one dared laugh at her stingy ways. She lived in a succession of modest rental houses—ten during her sixteen years in Los Angeles— taking them as is, with standard-issue furniture, moving on when her addresses were discovered by fans or by people at the studio. Between houses, the rootless Garbo stayed at the Beverly Hills Hotel or in a cottage at Chateau Marmont. When she at last did buy a house, in 1939, on Mayberry Road in Santa Monica, she furnished only two or three rooms and made spare provisions for guests. It was said that she would ask florists for day-old flowers, free for the taking; and that she returned magazines to news-stands after she'd flipped through them. The talk was that she kept detailed records of household accounts, and insisted that her domestic help adhere to a monthly budget of $100.

Garbo realized her value to her employers in January 1927, upon the release of her third MGM picture, *Flesh and the Devil.* In a day when a movie did well to run for a week, this first pairing of Garbo with John Gilbert broke month-long records across the country. The stars' on-camera lovemaking was not make-believe: So confided Clarence Brown, after directing the first of his eight Garbo films. "After I finished a scene with them," Brown said, "I felt like an intruder. I'd have to walk away, to let them finish what they were doing."

In the twenty-first century, *Flesh and the Devil* will still cause tingles, with the dominant Garbo taking Gilbert, holding his hand to her breast, and parting her lips to kiss him. They do it before a roaring fire, on a park bench, in front of an open boudoir window. Theirs is a wonderfully profane love, and Garbo is an unapolo-getic adulteress—sitting in a church pew, between her husband (Hanson) and her lover (Gilbert), she primps, even as the preacher, looking right at her, lashes out at the sin of adultery. At the communion rail, Garbo forcibly turns the chalice so that her lips will touch the same spot as her lover's. As she did in *The*

Garbo had only two responses to the Museum of Modern Art's 1968 retrospective of her films: "I think it's terrible that they're showing some of those," and a more heartfelt, "I don't get penny from it."

> *You're the top!...*
> *You're the National Gall'ry—*
> *You're Garbo's sal'ry,*
> *You're cellophane!*
>
> —COLE PORTER

One afternoon Sam Marx, the Metro story editor, sent a script via messenger to Garbo at her home in Santa Monica. At the end of the day, the messenger returned—script still in hand. He'd not been able to make the delivery. "He could hear laughter and music coming from inside the house," says Marx. "It was Cole Porter's 'You're the Top.' The kid rang the front bell, banged on the door, then went around back. If Garbo heard him, she wasn't letting him in. When he went to knock on a window, he peeked inside, and saw Garbo dancing with a woman friend of hers—they were playing a certain verse of the song over and over, laughing about the lyrics. He decided not to intrude."

*Torrent* and *The Temptress,* Garbo pays for her sins in the end, this time by falling through a hole in an icy lake. "In practically all the pictures assigned to the exquisite Greta Garbo," wrote Robert Sherwood, "she has been so inexcusably wicked that she could expiate her numerous errors only in death . . . by way of reminding the Girl Scouts of America just what the wages of sin [are]."

But even with the unhappy ending, the film was a hit. "Patrons wishing to see the picture," warned the *New York Times,* "[must] form lines at the Capitol Theatre extending to both Fiftieth and Fifty-first streets and half-way down those blocks." The fact did not escape Garbo that she was paid far less than the man with whom she shared billing. Though her weekly salary had been raised once, to $600, John Gilbert's was $10,000. Anticipating her discontent, Mayer called Garbo into his office and offered her $2,500. Hearing that, she went home and ignored calls from the studio. She wanted a raise, a big one, and she wanted roles that would assure her of a long career. "Four or five more bad pictures, and there would be no more of me left for the American people," said Garbo, who was tired of playing vamps. She also was just plain tired. "My constitution is not strong," she said. "If I were to play as many roles as they see fit I would break down under the strain." There was nothing for her to do but go on strike. She would have her way, or not work again.

She had done this before, but briefly, refusing to report to the set of the odious *Temptress* after Stiller was fired. "Believe me, that was a big scandal," Garbo wrote to her friend Lars Saxon in Stockholm. "They think I am mad! Oh, oh . . . People say that they are going to send me back home. I don't know what will happen." This time, Garbo stayed away for almost seven months, without pay, until Mayer capitulated. Her colleagues and fans were amazed. On June 1, 1927, Garbo signed a new five-year contract, giving her $7,500 per week, to be paid fifty-two weeks a year, whether she was working or not. An editorial cartoon that appeared later that week showed her holding bags of money. The contract also gave her approval of scripts, directors, and co-stars.

For the duration of her career, however, Garbo would not show much savvy in exercising those powers. Given the chance

*With Lars Hanson and Clarence Brown on the set of* Flesh and the Devil.

to work with Alfred Hitchcock and Laurence Olivier, for instance, she declined; and in her choices of script she usually opted for the more familiar, and less challenging. But for now, with a lucrative new contract in hand, Garbo was content to go back to work, and it would be a distinguished project. She would play Anna Karenina, though MGM insisted on retitling the Tolstoy: It would be Greta Garbo and John Gilbert in *Love*. Back at the studio at last, she found a bouquet of flowers in her dressing room, a welcome-home gift from the wardrobe department. The gesture, she said, "made me feel a little closer."

*I* went once on a freighter. I don't know what made me go on that month in solitude. I was a young strapping boy and I was leaving from Sweden, and I didn't have anyone, so I went alone. You're not completely alone if you're on a freighter—I mean, there's a captain and the sailors. The freighter took a month, I think, four weeks from Sweden to America. I didn't love it exactly, but I liked it. I went through the Panama Canal. I ate alone on the deck in a lifeboat. They brought me a little tray—I never went to the dining room. I liked being on the sea like that.

There was a storm one time and there was a huge deck for freight. I went down and walked. It was enormous—I walked and walked, and the captain came by and said, "My God, you're a good sailor!" because I was the only one out. The ship went up and down and I adored it. Had I been in the cabin I probably would have been ill.

Somewhere I got off alone and that was that.

Salka Viertel was there to meet "Harriet Brown" when the freighter *Annie Johnson* docked at San Diego one afternoon in 1932. "We hoped that she would disembark unnoticed," Viertel wrote, "[but] aggressive reporters . . . were determined not to leave . . . until she appeared. There was nothing to do but give in." Garbo had tried to get off at quarantine, but the captain couldn't allow it. She had been gone for two months, since completing the ambitious *As You Desire Me,* a movie that turns on the same is-she-or-isn't-she hinge as *Vertigo,* and it was rumored that she would not return—to California or to the movies. Taking her turn at the gangplank, Garbo managed a smile for the crowd and said, "I am very glad to be back." Asked about her plans, she was her usual vague self: "One never knows what time will bring, does one?"

In Sweden Garbo had been researching the life of Queen Christina, the seventeenth-century monarch, for a film that she and Viertel were eager to make. Garbo had visited the castle at Uppsala, studied portraits by Van Dyck and Velázquez (Christina had visited the Spanish court), and searched through palace archives made available to her by the royal family. She meant the film to be a tribute to her homeland, and felt kinship with the queen who said such things as "I would rather die than be married" and "I am the least curious in clothes of any woman." There are other parallels between Christina and Garbo, both of whom abdicated their exalted positions, referred to themselves in the masculine (Christina called herself "the king of Sweden"), and were intimate with men and women alike. Christina enjoyed disguising herself as a man and, being physically indelicate, did so successfully. (Garbo's disguise in *Queen Christina* is as unconvincing as Julie Andrews's in *Victor/Victoria.*) For all their good intentions in a pre-feminist age, the writers—Viertel, H. M. Harwood and S. N. Behrman—fell back on unenlightened notions of femininity while working out the scene in which Christina's lover discovers her true gender. Notes from a script conference:

> Business of the two of them washing their hands, jackets removed. The man washes his wrists, whereas the girl, very lightly, the fingers.
> Business of Antonio tossing a book of poems . . . to the girl, for her to catch. Her posture in catching would reveal her identity. . . .
> Christina's effort at trying to open a window might reveal her awkwardness to Antonio and the fact that she is a girl;
> Antonio might ask her to help him unlace an obstinate boot and the way she goes about it, kneeling down to untie the knot, might serve the purpose.

Garbo's insistence on co-starring with John Gilbert has been described as a gracious gesture on her part, an attempt to revive her old flame's career. She might also have hoped that their reunion would boost her box office, which had flagged with *As You Desire Me.* But the Garbo-Gilbert spark was cold, and *Queen Christina* is a stately thing, crushing her with "deathly reverence," said Graham Greene. "She is like a Tudor mansion set up again brick by numbered brick near Philadelphia." You didn't have to be Swedish to know the film had fictionalized the facts, but the distortions didn't make for a lively costume drama, either. Though the picture was considered an "intelligentsia success," at least one paper spoke out frankly for the time, criticizing it for not dealing straightforwardly with the queen's sexual ambiguity. "They have disregarded completely the intensity of Christina's devotion for [her] Countess," ran the *World-Telegram* review. Garbo liked much about the film, though she did apologize for its "terrible compromise," as she told reporters in Sweden. "It is difficult to be allowed to try anything. There's no time for art. All that matters is what they call box-office."

A year had passed when Metro released *The Painted Veil,* based on the novel by Somerset Maugham, which placed Garbo, as the unfaithful but repentant missionary's wife, in a thoroughly *moderne* Orient. A promotional letter to theater owners all but apologized for the deadbeat *Queen Christina:*

> This is THE Garbo of your fondest memories . . . of live, pulse-quickening memory—this woman is of warm flesh and warmer blood . . . of desire . . . and the courage to life and love and adventure. . . .
> Now Garbo goes back to her fans, to the great multitude that worship her. Garbo owes her box-office success to the mob, not the classes. . . .
> This is the kind of picture you can sell with Garbo!

Except for a dinner-party scene in which Garbo, seated between her husband and her lover, barely keeps a lid on her emotions, *The Painted Veil* is dull, and it elicited more criticism of the loved her–hated it variety. "She triumphs by the sheer beauty of herself," said Norman Lusk in *Picture Play.* "[The] picture . . . is only tolerable because of what she gives to it."

Opposite: *Royalty plays royalty and ponders the throne: Garbo as Queen Christina.*

75

Laurence Olivier, ne to Hollywood, was th studio's first choice co-star in *Queen Christina,* but was dismissed after Garl complained that the chemistry was not right. Olivier graciously took the blame, calling himse "a mouse to her lioness."

Garbo was shy about rehearsing, but Rouben Mamoulian managed to convince her of its value while making *Queen Christina* with John Gilbert and Lewis Stone:

"When I started, Garbo told me that she couldn't rehearse, that I should rehearse other people, then she'd walk in and do the scene and we'd photograph it.... She said that I would find that she could not rehearse, and if she did the results would be very bad....

"I said, 'Well, I'm quite open on this, so let's do it both ways. Let's do a scene without a rehearsal, and then let's do it with a rehearsal.'

"I rehearsed the other actors, then Miss Garbo stepped into the scene, and we made a take. I asked her how she felt about it, and she said, 'Fine.' She asked me how I felt about it and I said I didn't feel good at all, that it was not right. So she got very discouraged and said, 'What are we going to do?' I said, 'We have to rehearse.' She said, 'Let's take a chance.'

"So we rehearsed for an hour and for another hour and for another hour and she said, 'You know, you'll get nothing out of me, it's all terrible.' I said, 'No, it's better all the time.'

"So finally we started making a take—the second take, the third and I was satisfied with the eighth."

Mamoulian gave Garbo the choice—between the first take, made with no rehearsal, and the eighth.

"She was very cute. She leaned down and whispered, 'Do not print the first take.'"

*Garbo's films always enjoyed a large European box office.*

Mayer's son-in-law, David O. Selznick, was given the honor and the challenge of producing Garbo's next picture. He was convinced that she must do something sharp and contemporary, and he knew just the property, too—*Dark Victory*. Anyone familiar with the Bette Davis weeper may have trouble imagining Garbo as Judith Traherne, the horsey debutante who so nobly meets her doom. But Selznick intended to adapt the character to Garbo, making her the daughter of an American heiress and a European nobleman. Jock Whitney owned the play, which had a short run on Broadway with Tallulah Bankhead, and there was talk at MGM of snapping it up for Katharine Hepburn. (This was indeed a hot property—when Harry Cohn refused to buy the play for Gloria Swanson when she was under contract to Columbia, she yanked the telephone out of the wall.)

Selznick got George Cukor excited about directing Garbo in the picture, and the two men made their approach.

But Garbo wasn't interested—she wanted to do *Anna Karenina,* only talking this time (she had starred in the silent version, *Love,* in 1927). That said, she went off to Palm Springs. In an overnight letter to her, Selznick was blunt about his "lack of enthusiasm and instinct of dread" for the project:

> I was extremely sorry to hear this morning that you had left [for vacation], because we must arrive at an immediate decision, which, I think, will have a telling effect on your entire career. . . . I, personally, feel that . . . to do a heavy Russian drama on the heels of so many ponderous, similar films, in which [people] have seen you and other stars recently, would prove to be a mistake. I still think *Karenina* can be a magnificent film and I would be willing to make it with you later, but to do it now, following upon the disappointment of *Christina* and *The Painted Veil,* is something I dislike contemplating. . . .
>
> I request and most earnestly urge you to permit us to switch from *Anna Karenina* to *Dark Victory.*

Garbo wouldn't budge, but Selznick continued brainstorming with story editor Kate Corbaley and an aspiring writer in her department, Val Lewton, hoping to find a lively alternative to *Karenina.* They considered the strange new Noel Coward, *Point Valaine,* about the proprietress of a Caribbean inn and her suicidal headwaiter. (Starring Alfred Lunt, Lynn Fontanne, and the author, it had lasted only a few weeks on Broadway; one critic, torturing Coward for boasting that he wrote his plays while on his travels, accused him of writing this one on a train between New York and Philadelphia.)

Selznick and company grasped at anything, contemporary and upbeat or not. Garbo as Nicole Diver in Fitzgerald's *Tender Is the Night* made it to the memo stage. Shakespeare was discussed: *Much Ado About Nothing,* with Garbo and Clark Gable as Beatrice and Benedick, and *Hamlet.* The latter might have appealed to Garbo if she and not Leslie Howard had been proposed for the title role—she wasn't interested in playing Ophelia. (Dressed in black, Garbo had come as Hamlet to a masquerade given by Basil Rathbone at the Beverly Hills Hotel the night of October 27, 1929. She arrived alone, never removed her eye mask, and left undetected, apparently deriving much pleasure from the intrigue.)

Selznick vetoed Isadora Duncan's autobiography, *My Life,* as being "too censorable" and because it would present Garbo in another "sacrificial, woebegone aspect." A biography of Mary, Queen of Scots was rejected in a script reader's report as "really a modern gangster play . . . Stuart is the female Al Capone of her time." Selznick's team thought that Willa Cather's *My Ántonia* or Conrad's *Arrow of Gold* would make a fascinating match of author and actor, with Garbo playing Cather's immigrant prairie heroine or Conrad's introspective lady of Marseilles. But no, she said. Even *Jezebel* made the list, but apparently Garbo couldn't see herself as antebellum spitfire. She countered with *Tovarich,* a crowd-pleasing play about two aristocratic Russian refugees zanily coping with their reduced circumstances. Selznick didn't like that idea, and Garbo's original wish prevailed: They would do *Anna Karenina.*

Some of Garbo's fans agreed that she had played enough lugubrious historical roles (but they didn't realize it was she who had been resisting the twentieth century). In *Hollywood Magazine,* one Garbomaniac decried the star's "terrible waste," and advised filmmakers of what Garbo "really needs to wring the withers of the whole world: a jersey, a rough-and-ready skirt or trousers, untidy hair, and the guttural of her voice. Pitch her into a cod-smelling Stockholm bar or a misty-wreathed waterfront. Against such a background she could act a masterpiece."

Though he lost his argument with Garbo, Selznick's production of *Anna Karenina* was not begrudging. Metro lavishly recreated landmarks of St. Petersburg, including a cathedral and opera house, a railway station, a half-dozen palatial houses, and, according to the studio, "the largest ballroom ever made for a movie." Adrian designed white ball gowns and hooded furs for Garbo, and Selznick enlisted Erich von Stroheim and Andrey Tolstoy as technical advisers—Stroheim for military details, Tolstoy for the legitimacy his name would lend to the production of his distant relative's masterpiece. Garbo did not get her first choice of director, George Cukor, who bowed out after reading the screenplay, which he pronounced boring. She surprised no one by calling in Clarence Brown as his replacement. The film focuses only on the novel's personal tragedy, but it does so well enough, even as compromised by censorship regulations that forbade "adultery without remorse." By Production Code standards, even Anna's suicide on the train tracks did not show sufficient contrition, because she had willingly left her husband to enjoy herself with Vronsky. (In a guide to the movie provided for "adult study groups," Selznick lashed out at "fanatical censorship restrictions... that make no discrimination between Tolstoy and pennyshockers.")

Though Selznick knew he had some strong performances and a sumptuous setting, he still worried that the picture would lumber like a dinosaur, and was convinced that its most promising box-office lure was little Freddie Bartholomew, the lovable *David Copperfield* star who as Anna's son has some touching scenes with Garbo. Even Fredric March, who played Count Vronsky and was never quite charmed by Garbo, conceded that she "had a wonderful way with all children." In a memo to his promotion and advertising departments, Selznick wrote: "Imagine a production with Garbo and Shirley Temple. That's how it should be sold.... [Don't] dish it out as another *Christina* or *Painted Veil.*" He also thought it wise to make no reference to the silent *Love,* "as there might seem to be a staleness to the subject."

But when *Anna Karenina* opened in September of 1935, Garbo was vindicated: As she appears through a cloud of steam at the beginning of the picture, first-day audiences at the Capitol Theatre cheered. Like most reviewers, *Variety*'s found the movie slow ("elephantine," in fact) but also conceded that Garbo "never had a part which suited her more comfortably... it is strawberry jam to [her] toast." Maureen O'Sullivan, who played Kitty in the film, admitted that she simply could not see what was so special about Garbo as they played scenes together: "I thought, 'If that's what the studio is so excited about, well, they must be mad.' I thought Garbo was terrible—not doing a thing while the rest of us acted up a storm around her. But then I saw the rushes, and Garbo had made fools of all of us. She was the only one who stood out and made the scenes believable."

Despite their horn-locking at the beginning of the project, Garbo appreciated Selznick's handling of the production and hoped he would produce her next picture. But he was to leave Metro, to form Selznick International.

After the success of *Anna Karenina,* for which Garbo won the New York Film Critics Award for Best Actress, came her apotheosis in *Camille.* The performance won her a second New York Film Critics Award, an Oscar nomination, and the greatest critical acclaim of her career. The Bernhardt-Duse torch was now Garbo's, a neat accomplishment for an actress whose habit had been to triumph over substandard material. George Cukor, who had balked at *Anna Karenina,* was eager to direct this "happy meeting of an actress and a part." During the production, Garbo kept her distance from her boyish co-star Robert Taylor—not because she didn't like him (she cried when she heard the news of his death from cancer in 1969)—but in order to maintain the tension that must exist between lovers. "She had to believe that he was the ideal young man," Cukor said, "and . . . not just another nice kid."

In 1963, the Royal Ballet mounted Frederick Ashton's production of Dumas's *La Dame aux Camillias.* Called "Marguerite and Armand," the ballet was a beautiful showcase for Margot Fonteyn and Rudolf Nureyev (the decor was by Cecil Beaton), and at Valentina and George Schlee's invitation, Garbo attended the premiere at the Metropolitan Opera House. She didn't like it, but then Garbo didn't much like any ballet. "Those poor fellows," she said, "having to lift all those big girls. It's so silly."

The film remains a vibrant, intriguing love story—and will endure for many generations. "The last thing any actress should want to do, ever, is to remake *Camille,*" said Joseph L. Mankiewicz, "because whether or not she is better than Miss Garbo . . . no one will ever admit it, or could admit it, because she would be competing with a myth, a memory. The point is that Garbo, who was great, becomes greater every year, in memory."

Metro's reverence toward Garbo was now unqualified. No other star was treated quite so gingerly, and the kid-glove etiquette that developed around her turned the studio into a sort of Versailles, where she was queen. She was always "Miss Garbo," even to those who worked with her regularly and to the few who also saw her socially. Clarence Brown claimed that he never gave her a direction above a whisper (and it is impossible to imagine anyone barking at Garbo through a megaphone). While directing her in *Ninotchka,* in which she so gamely sends up her own dour self, Ernst Lubitsch devised a little ritual, donning a coat and tie to greet the star each morning at her dressing-room door. Between scenes, she would retire to her quarters, to lie down in the dark until Lubitsch summoned her with a soft buzzer. Though he worked in shirtsleeves and open collar, he spruced up again before stopping by her dressing room to say good night each evening. Perhaps all the deference occasionally got to Garbo; she seemed amused when gruffly put through paces by Woody Van Dyke, a no-nonsense team player who directed films as varied as *Tarzan the Ape Man, The Thin Man,* and *Marie Antoinette.* According to the English director Michael Powell, Van Dyke had been asked to handle some retakes of an entrance and exit:

> Van Dyke was seated in his chair looking at the script of the film. [Garbo] said, "Good morning." He said, "Mornin' honey," without looking up. "The script says you come through that door"—pointing to the top of the stairs—"and you go out that door"—pointing to the door across the splendid baroque hall at the bottom of the staircase. . . . She went up the stairs and went through the action: "How was that?" "Swell. Now the script says you have a change of costume and you come in that door and go out the other." She was puzzled . . . and looked at him.

"Mister Van Dyke, don't you ever rehearse?" He was already back in the script and answered without raising his eyes: "Listen, honey, how many ways are there of coming down a staircase?"

As Rouben Mamoulian had discovered, Garbo rehearsed with other actors only when absolutely necessary, preferring to learn her lines and work through her characterizations on her own, blocking scenes with fellow players just before shooting. She prepared herself meticulously, and apologized profusely if ever she forgot her lines. Sam Marx says that everyone at MGM, from Mayer and Thalberg down, regarded her as a "consummate actress, a complete and total professional." She might have been the ultimate Method actor, intuitive and internal, but the few comments she ever made about her craft are self-effacing and dismissive, and suggest that her genius was as much of a mystery to herself as to anyone:

"If I don't feel a line I can't act. . . . I don't even have to look the part—I just have to feel it."

"I didn't like to know what the lines meant. I did anything that came into my head and made a kind of fantasy of it, but I never knew what I was doing, and I didn't want to know the people I was acting with. . . . I didn't ever know what it was all about."

Lewis Stone, who made more movies with Garbo than any other actor (from *A Woman of Affairs* to *Queen Christina*), said that she "never got over stage fright. It tied her up in knots and made her seem antisocial, aloof. She suffered like the dickens, I'm sure of that."

An actress who has a near-phobia about rehearsing and who cannot stand to be looked at has made as unlikely a career choice as a lighthouse keeper who hates being alone. Garbo, in fact, would have made a fine lighthouse keeper; but here she was, working among thousands of other employees. Closed sets were not unheard of, but Garbo's were like top-secret laboratories. Anyone not required for the task—actors, technicians, assistants (including workers high up on catwalks)—had to withdraw.

Her ability to detect an unauthorized presence on the set was uncanny, like a sixth sense. Lionel Barrymore likened her to "a cat that crawls under the bed when a stranger comes into the

Opposite: *A hushed conference with Clarence Brown during the making of* Anna Karenina.

room." He was present on the set of *Grand Hotel* when Louis B. Mayer allowed Arthur Brisbane, the mighty Hearst editor, to slip into the sound booth to watch from above. Garbo abruptly broke off a scene, went to her dressing room, and made it clear that she could not resume work until the trespasser had left. Told whom she had evicted, Garbo shrugged and said, "I wouldn't look over his shoulder while he's writing an editorial." Though some must have found her demands tiresome, John Barrymore defended Garbo. "She didn't do it to be snotty," he said. "She would have done the same thing had it been Jesus Christ."

Large black screens, called flats, sometimes were placed around Garbo (and the essential cast members and crew), not so much to isolate her but to block out distractions. "It really started with sound," said Clarence Brown, who may have been Garbo's favorite director precisely because he accommodated her to the extreme, agreeing to perform his (whispered) duties through cracks in the flats. "In the silent days, we had hard lights [and] you couldn't see beyond them, couldn't see the cameramen. . . . But with sound, we developed fast film [that] used incandescent lighting, not much more light than you'd use in a drawing room. With that light, Garbo could see the set and it kept her from concentrating on her acting. Her eye would pass around the set and a person would be staring at her, thinking, 'So this is the great Garbo.' She'd stop acting and start looking back at the eyes. When she finished she'd look at me and say, 'Oh, those people.' Finally we put screens up around the set."

Brown wasn't the only one to take extraordinary care with Garbo. "There are eight thousand intrusions while a picture is being made," said George Cukor. "All acting is concentration [and] Garbo had real, real intensity." Garbo believed, as Cukor put it, "in real illusion," which is why she found it difficult to look at rushes. "She would have some ideal picture in her mind of what she was doing," said Cukor, "and would never allow that to be destroyed. She was never pleased with what she saw on the screen." When Cukor asked Garbo why an audience made her so uncomfortable, she replied, "If people are watching, I'm just a woman making faces in front of a camera." (She echoed herself years later, huddled with David Niven under a picnic table during a sudden rainstorm on the French Riviera. Niven seized the moment, raising the forbidden question: Why had she left the movies? "Because," Garbo said after a long pause, "I had made enough faces.")

After she had stopped working, Garbo kept a deliberate distance from her screen self. The few times she is known to have sat through her films—with Allen Porter, at the Museum of Modern Art, and with other friends, sometimes in MGM projection rooms—Garbo seemed to forget who she was watching on the screen, referring to herself in the third person. Jane Gunther remembers a private screening of *Anna Karenina* arranged by

*"She is a great lady and a great actress and the rest is silence," said John Barrymore of Garbo, who made just one picture with her. According to some accounts, when she met Barrymore on the set of* Grand Hotel, *Garbo threw her arms around him and told him how grateful she was to at last work with "a real artist." Barrymore later wrote that he was forever grateful to Garbo for sharing her (still) secret hangover remedy with him.*

Garbo in California for her late husband, the journalist John Gunther. As the three sat watching, Garbo would say, "Look now, she's about to do this," or "Oh, she wasn't very good in that scene, was she?"

For all her aura of untouchability at the studio, if the proper etiquette was observed, Garbo was entirely approachable and not at all given to displays of temperament. She was in fact down-to-earth on the job, friendly to extras, at ease with the men in their shirtsleeves. She never berated anyone, and no one has ever reported an angry outburst. When an assistant in Clarence Bull's studio knocked over a spotlight, smacking her on the shoulder, Garbo laughed it off and the next day greeted him with a light-hearted, "Been trying to kill anyone lately?" When, on another occasion, a heavy piece of scenery came crashing down near her, she looked up at the mortified prop boy and purred, "I make you nervous, maybe?" Clarence Brown recalled her sweet way with a young Irishman on a crew, "an electrician, and his face looked like the map of Ireland. Garbo used to kid him all the time. She'd say to him, 'Are you Scandinavian?' " She adored William Daniels's gaffer, Bill Porter, who stood next to her in close-ups, lighting her eyes. At the end of those intense scenes, Garbo would gently touch Porter as she walked back to her dressing room. "She was peculiar but marvelous," said Porter, "[and] very friendly. She always felt at home with me."

Garbo was the unusual star who was mostly punctual and did not travel in an entourage. "If she said she was going to be there at nine o'clock," said Clarence Bull, describing a photography session with Garbo, "you could expect her at ten minutes to nine. And she never brought anyone with her, didn't want anyone around." Garbo's punctuality extended to quitting time, which was the stroke of five p.m. "An actress is no good after eight hours on the set," Garbo told Elizabeth Young, who played the countess to her Queen Christina. Many accounts have Garbo stopping a scene, even in mid-sentence, when her dressing room attendant, Alma, arrives on the set with a cup of tea, marking the end of the work day. As the star once said of her punctual assistant, "Making a picture without Alma is like being in New York without dark glasses."

Transfixed by the Grand Kabuki, which she saw on its first American tour in 1960, Garbo asked if she could go backstage to watch the transformation of men into women. The company manager's answer was a Garboesque no: "Let her be content with the illusion."

# 4 THE VOICE

*I* wish I could speak any language. It's asinine to say things the way I do. If you can't express yourself . . . It's my English—I don't stipulate words as I should. I don't get things very straight. Unique? Well, that doesn't mean you should be so unique that no one can understand you, that you can't learn something, that you say things like I do and don't mean to.

One has to be an idiot to talk to me, no matter where I am. They mustn't find out that I don't know about grammar in any language. I don't speak grammar in any language, including the language I was born with.

Garbo's difficulty with English exacerbated her natural shyness and burdened her at Metro: Imagine taking direction from men whose hurried commands—"Left," "Right," "Enter," "Exit" —confuse you; or being fitted for costumes by seamstresses, mumbling through pins in their mouths, ordering you to turn this way and that. Cameraman William Daniels took kindly to this frightened, far-from-home girl. "It took her a time to speak English, and she was shy, *so* shy," said Daniels, who claimed it was his idea, unprecedented at any studio, to shield Garbo from all visitors, closing her sets even to top studio officials. "I did it to protect her . . . [from] a bunch of staring, gum-chewing, whispering people." Daniels also occasionally helped Garbo with her English, and was on the set of *The Torrent* when she suddenly blurted out, "Garbo important. Garbo important!" Daniels claimed it was the first time that she had spoken up in any language; stunned, he rushed to her side, assuring her that yes, she was important, the most important person there, in fact. But she continued: "Important Garbo, important sardines—all the same." She was making a little joke, at her expense: Playing a Spanish prima donna who drives men to madness, in a film she denounced in a letter home as "rotten—beneath criticism," Garbo felt like an ordinary imported commodity.

At the picture's Hollywood premiere, Garbo was introduced by director Monta Bell, to whom she was "a human enigma . . . far removed from the normal American makeup." Also brought on stage was Antonio Moreno, her love victim in *The Temptress*, which was already shooting. Bell apologized to the audience for Garbo's silence, explaining that she could speak no English. "Can you?" he asked, turning to Garbo, who solemnly gave her rehearsed answer: "Not one word." Everyone laughed.

What's the expression? I was down on Thirty-fourth Street today, and wanted to run another errand—what do you call that, when you can do two things at once? Get two birdies with one whatever it is . . . isn't there an expression? Two birdies in one . . . That's it: Two birdies with one stone. It's exhausting to talk like I do.

Contradicting the William Daniels story, it was also widely reported that Garbo's first English word, muttered during a fitting for *The Torrent*, was "applesauce," as in "Oh, applesauce!" (the "baloney" or "bullshit" of the day). Another tale had her mustering "Beat it!" to a Metro guard who reprimanded her for picking figs from a tree on the back lot. *Silver Screen* claimed that Garbo's first utterance in English was prompted by Ricardo Cortez, when he asked his *Torrent* co-star her opinion of California: "Ah, hell," Garbo drawled, according to the magazine. The writer added that "her fascinating mouth labor[ed] over the unfamiliar word."

The studios were accustomed to running defense for foreign stars who spoke little English, or garbled it, making foolish or unintentionally funny statements. But Howard Strickling, head of MGM's West Coast publicity office, recognized a severe case when Garbo stepped off the *Twentieth Century Limited* in Pasadena on September 10, 1925. Strickling had drummed up a dozen or so reporters and photographers, as well as a contingent of transplanted Scandinavians to make the newcomers feel at home and to facilitate communication. Wearing her trusty checked traveling suit and clinging to Mauritz Stiller, Garbo said two lines in English she'd practiced all the way from New York: "This is the happiest day of my life. God bless America." Asked where she would like to live, she said through an interpreter, "I hope to find a room with a nice private family somewhere." It wasn't a wow of a quote, the sort of cute thing that young hopefuls were coached to say, and MGM eyeballs must have rolled. Garbo was Eliza Doolittle, piping up at Ascot, and Strickling was the mortified Henry Higgins, putting a teacup on his head.

*I* speak a little English because I live here.

Though Mauritz Stiller had advised Garbo against talking to journalists (during the filming of *The Saga of Gösta Berling,* she revealed in a Swedish newspaper—much to the director's disliking—that "being feminine is a lovely quality which I may not have very much of"), Metro pressed her to do so. In interviews she came across not as bewitchingly strange, as the studio had hoped, but as off-puttingly so, and readers didn't know what to think when she came out with such clinkers as "In America you are all so happy. Why are you so happy all the time? I am not always happy. Sometimes yes, sometimes no. When I am angry, I am very bad. I shut my door and do not speak."

Her employers, in fact, began to wish she wouldn't speak, and it was decided that a studio official must be present at all interviews. That was fine with Garbo, who was beginning "to feel like a circus horse." At about the same time, late 1926, Lon Chaney stole onto the set of *The Temptress* and allegedly whispered to Garbo, "Mystery has served me well—it could do the same for you." If the story is true—and a photograph does exist of Chaney, in costume for *The Road to Mandalay,* taking Garbo's hand—she must have cherished the moment, for she admired the actor's artistry and his disdain for celebrity. She also fancied the example

Garbo's manner was misunderstood by most everyone, according to Douglas Fairbanks, Jr., who played her wild-eyed wastrel brother in *A Woman of Affairs*. "Her silence gave the impression that she was unfriendly or felt superior," says Fairbanks, who stayed in touch with Garbo over the years. "But it was only shyness. She was simply Scandinavian, and they're an extremely reserved bunch of people. Her way with the press never struck me as an attempt to be difficult—she just wasn't an exhibitionist, and in Hollywood, in that business, that was unusual. People didn't know what to make of it."

of Maude Adams, the New York stage actress who made a long career playing Peter Pan and other James M. Barrie characters, and who adopted a theatrically mysterious manner, riding around town in a horse-drawn carriage with curtains drawn.

*Fairbanks and Garbo as gorgeous brother and sister.*

After the phenomenal celebrity of her third picture, *Flesh and the Devil,* Garbo balked at more vamping, refusing the next steamer prepared for her, *Women Love Diamonds* (Pauline Starke took the forgettable role). The news ran through town that the Swede was tired of playing "wicked women," though she had pronounced the *w*'s as *v*'s and mangled the plural: "vicked vomens." James Quirk, the editor of *Photoplay,* took MGM's side and also a mean little swipe at Garbo: "For the love of Thomas Alva Edison, gal . . . when you learn to speak English, inquire how many beautiful and clever girls have been absolutely ruined by playing good women without ever having a chance to show how bad they could be. Some actresses would give a year's salary if they could once be permitted to play a hell-raising, double-crossing, censor-teaser for six reels."

When Louis B. Mayer insisted that she take the roles offered her, Garbo made her historic reply: "I think I go home." That didn't mean back to Stockholm, just back to her hotel room in

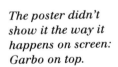

*The poster didn't
show it the way it
happens on screen:
Garbo on top.*

Santa Monica, to which she summoned Harry Edington, John Gilbert's savvy manager. Garbo, going on strike for better scripts and more money, described Edington as "somebody who could talk the English language [for me]. He saw how sick I was, how tired." Though studio heads fought Edington on most points in his negotiations on her behalf, they did not flinch when he called an end to virtually all publicity, including promotional photographs and appearances at premieres. From now on, Garbo would be photographed only in the studio and in character, keeping her that much more remote and unknowable. (A comradely cast photograph from the set of *Grand Hotel* has been cited as an exception to the rule, but the picture clearly is doctored, with Garbo pasted in between Joan Crawford and John Barrymore.)

As for interviews, only Garbo would determine where and when she would speak, if ever.

It happened less than a year later, in a sort of swan song to the press that was also intended to show that Garbo, after returning to work after her walkout, was not a temperamental or greedy thing. For someone who hated talking about herself, she did so revealingly in a remarkable interview that ran in three consecutive issues of *Photoplay* in the spring of 1928. Here is Hollywood's

most exotic and fragile flower, vibrantly open one moment, droopy and closed the next. Who else but Garbo would begin her only major interview with a heartfelt "Let's not talk of me!"? She struggles to sound ordinary, but Garbo's conversation was like no one else's:

*The all-star cast of* Grand Hotel, *made complete by a pasted-in cut-out Garbo.*

> I was born; I grew up; I have lived like every other person. Why must people talk about me?
>
> We all do the same things in ways that are just a little different. We go to school, we learn; we are bad at times; we are good at others. But we grow up, the one the same as the other. We find our life work and we do it. That's all there is to anyone's life story, isn't it?
>
> Some people were born in red brick houses, others in

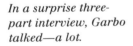

*In a surprise three-part interview, Garbo talked—a lot.*

plain white board ones. What is the difference? We were all born in houses.

I don't like many people. . . . I need to be alone, always. When I was just a little child, as early as I can remember, I have wanted to be alone. . . . I used to crawl into a corner and sit and think things over.

I have always been moody, very happy one moment, the next moment—there was nothing left for me.

Joe Cohn, Metro's general production manager and Louis B. Mayer's right hand, was at the studio when Garbo arrived and remembers that there was nothing manufactured about her timidity. "She was that way from the very beginning, when she was nineteen years old," says Cohn, now in his nineties. "There was nothing Garbo could do about the publicity we forced on her at first, and we tried a lot of different poses, none of them too smart. She didn't complain, but she wasn't enthusiastic, either. The practice was to present a new star as a certain type, so audiences would know what to expect. But it turned out that we couldn't do that with her. We didn't know it at first, but she was a genuine recluse—the general impression people have about her is that she developed into one, but that was something true within her."

My brother's name? My sister's? What does that matter? They are my people. Why should I tell their names to other people? Names do not matter.

It was a sad, strange, and fascinating confessional, and Garbo's closing words indicated it would be her last: "My little story of my life in pictures—of my whole life as far as that matters—is finished."

The ban on publicity only intensified the generally crazed curiosity about Garbo, and if she hadn't run from notepads and flashbulbs, fewer stories and photographs would have appeared. Part of her was playing a sulky child's game of hide-and-seek, running into closets, hoping to be found. Certainly her behavior made her more conspicuous. Eleanor Phillips Colt, *Vogue*'s West Coast editor for some thirty years, rode every morning at the Bel Air Stables and one morning encountered Garbo hiking up the bridle path. "She was in her trench coat and hat," says Colt, who married the producer Sammy Colt, Ethel Barrymore's son. "Unmistakable who it was. When she saw that someone was coming, she suddenly ran over to a bush and stuck her head down in it— just like an ostrich. Her feet and body were in the path, her head down, stuck in the bush. Really like an ostrich. You couldn't miss her."

Reticent and rarely seen, Garbo caused more excitement than if she'd been lolling poolside at the Beverly Hills Hotel, dispensing quotes. As Billy Wilder put it, "She said nothing, and let the world write her story." Garbo spoke not, never posed for the cover of any magazine, ran from klieg lights—and still the stories ava-

*Clarence Bull created the "Swedish Sphinx" and Garbo liked the joke. "Her silence," said Adela Rogers St. Johns, "was having nothing to say."*

lanched: Garbo Moving Again! Garbo Speeds Through Arizona Desert. Garbo—a.k.a. Harriet Brown—Goes for Jazz. Scandinavian Princess Sneaks into Preview. Garbo Fears Crowds. Not in Love, Says Garbo. Rain Makes Quiet Swede Happy. The gentlemanly press agent Harry Crocker, a friend of Garbo's despite his profession, once observed that entire columns were written about *not* getting an interview with the star—such as one by a gumshoe journalist who tailed Garbo and her friend the director Jacques

Feyder to a "subterranean cafe" in Los Angeles's Spanish Quarter, then to a racy revue, where he slipped into a seat *behind* Garbo to "study her face."

Bogus stories appeared, some generated by MGM in an attempt to humanize the "Swedish Sphinx." Declared one missive from Metro: "Garbo goes to symphony concerts. Garbo goes to ballets. Garbo goes to lectures. But she doesn't dress in ermine and jewels. She doesn't sit in box seats or leave her place at intermission. She sits . . . in the general audience and studies her program." It was reported that she took an undignified tumble at a Hollywood roller rink; that she drank lemonade in the summer; had a chow named Fimsy, a gray alley cat called Lion, and a parrot (Polly, naturally) that said, "Hello, Greta!" when the actress got home from a hard day's work.

Not surprisingly, Garbo's aloofness came to be resented, and one disgruntled correspondent struck back by making insinuations about her sexual preferences. "Even the people who inspired Garbo's seclusion and silence are a bit fed up," ran the unsigned item in *Screen Book,* which mistook Garbo's reclusiveness as a studio gimmick. "They welcome an exotic who can be both seen and heard in private life. An exotic who is warmly human . . . who enjoys life [and] who obeys natural feminine impulses."

During her years at the studio and after, Garbo, who never married and had no children, never bothered to contradict harmless conjecture about her life, though she did deny rumors of marriage: to John Gilbert; Prince Sigvard of Sweden, as well as his rich bachelor friend Wilhelm Sorensen; Eric de Rothschild-Goldschmidt; Rouben Mamoulian; Leopold Stokowski. Her brief companionship with the married Stokowski shared front-page billing with European war news in 1938, and the nonsense about a romance between them repelled Garbo, who gave a noncommital, indeed passionless comment on her relationship with the conductor: "He has seen much of the world's beauty and I had hoped to learn about such things from him." Privately Garbo was dismissive of Stokowski, who, after the success of *Fantasia,* grew increasingly enamored of Hollywood and café society—and with being seen at Garbo's side. After she had been spotted in a series of southwestern motels with Rouben Mamoulian, after their work together on *Queen Christina,* Garbo's byline ran beneath an article called "Why I Will Never Marry." Whoever did write the piece leaves the question of matrimony open, but attributes the actress's single status to her career, asking, "Can you imagine a man being known as Mr. Garbo and nothing else?"

**M**any people make me nervous. They're a little hectic and I'm a funny person. They want to emphasize things: "Isn't it *marvelous?*" or this or that, instead of being quiet. It isn't the talk. It's the way they emphasize things that makes me nervous. It's not necessary to be emphatic always. One can be very quiet with human beings and still talk, but if they constantly say, "Oh, isn't it *great* to be out?" or "Isn't it a *wonderful* day?" then I think the other person is not at ease.

After a long hiatus, the last rumor of marriage bubbled up in 1985, linking Garbo to her junior friend Sam Green, a New York art dealer. Green swore he had nothing to do with the gossip, which appeared in bold print in the *Globe* and other tabloids. Nonetheless, Garbo abruptly stopped returning his telephone calls, and made it known through their mutual friend Cecile de Rothschild that as far as she was concerned, he no longer existed. "She wasn't really foolish enough to believe that I planted the marriage story," says Green. "Really—if I had wanted to link our names that way, I wouldn't have chosen to do it in the scandal sheets." But Green insists he is not bitter about the incident. "It was all too sad to get angry about," he says. "She was in the process of closing herself off from everyone who really mattered to her. She probably always operated that way, but it had gotten worse as she got older. She must have thought that the fewer people she had around her, the fewer her responsibilities. The headlines about us gave her a reason to have one less person to deal with. By telling herself she'd been betrayed, she was able to cut me off without looking back."

And then I get nervous, because I don't like uneasy things. I'm better off alone, because I happen to be a human being born with an extremely thin skin, and that's not very good in this world.

And I can't stand people who hum. The moment there's a little pause, they start humming. Once I saw a couple, they

were newly married, hadn't been married more than a month, I think, and when there was a slight pause, either one of them started to hum. And I said, "Oh boy, that's not going to last."

Studio camaraderie is easy, and when pictures were silent—and sets didn't have to be—it could be rowdy. But Garbo would have none of it. "I cannot stand it for someone to come up and say, 'What did you think of the football game?'" she once complained. "Then I cannot get back on track, I cannot do my best work then."

During the photography sessions that followed the completion of her films, Clarence Bull turned on the radio in his studio to distract Garbo with music and to make the day-long task go more quickly. As he clicked off some ninety exposures, Garbo would sing along with the popular songs; her somber rendition of "I Want to Be Happy" made Bull, and herself, laugh out loud. Once, when an announcer interrupted the music with chatter, Garbo blurted out, "What on earth is that man talking about—how can anybody talk so much about anything? What can it be that means so many words?"

After completing *Inspiration*, Robert Montgomery had to face the inevitable question from reporters: What is *she* really like? "Making a film with Garbo doesn't constitute an introduction," Montgomery replied.

A friend in Paris said to me, "Now really, it's unpardonable that you're doing nothing, and couldn't you at least learn a little French?" My friends in Paris are spoiled people—they have no patience with people who don't speak the language there. They get bored stiff.

It's true—if you're cultivated, cultured at all, you ought to speak French, but then I am not, so I can't. I speak a little French when the spirit moves me, but it doesn't mean I speak French. It's an involved language. And the French speak so fast, you don't know what language they're speaking.

You know what I always thought I'd like to do is go to Berlitz, but I need to find some private person I suppose. I could learn French easily if I could have somebody teach it to me. You have to sit down like a little child and try to learn it. If somebody just came hopping down from the sky then perhaps I would learn something. I don't know why it can't be like English, then I could understand it. I could learn from records—I have a phonograph, but I'm afraid to use it.

I have an amazing capacity for evading the whole business. Well, *je ne suis pas sûr de rien* [I'm not sure of anything].

Though her first MGM scripts were translated for her, Garbo was rarely without her Swedish-English lexicon, and she soon started language lessons, studying with tutors assigned by the studio to foreign players. One was a fellow Swede, Sven Borg, but apparently her favorite teacher was a black woman, whose name is not known. When talking pictures arrived, language tutors and diction coaches became important members of production teams, summoned to help players, home-grown and imported, who now had to give voice to their emotional displays. As *Singin' in the Rain* so wonderfully demonstrates, movies suddenly were no place for actors who squeaked or twanged when they spoke, and many suffered the fate of the outrageously shrill star, Lena Lamont. One well-known casualty was Vilma Banky, whose yowling in *A Lady to Love* struck one critic as "a strange mixture of Budapest and Chicago." Emil Jannings, who spoke with a heavy German accent, returned home.

Audiences who had swooned at the sight of John Gilbert giggled when they heard him speak in 1929's *His Glorious Night*. But the fall of this idol, as a fantastic conspiracy theory has it, may have been the doing of his archenemy and employer, Louis B. Mayer. Gilbert's enormous salary and his flagrant, wild-hair ways had long aggravated Mayer, and the two men came to blows on September 8, 1926. Garbo was the catalyst. The occasion was the marriage of the actress Eleanor Boardman to the director King Vidor, which was meant to be a double ceremony with Garbo and Gilbert. Everyone gathered at the seaside home of Marion Davies for the occasion—everyone but Garbo, and, according to Boardman, Mayer began taunting the jilted Gilbert. "It was a terrible scene," says Boardman. "Jack lunged at Mr. Mayer, knocking him onto the tile floor. After that, Mr. Mayer looked at Jack and told him, 'You'll pay for this, if it costs me millions, you'll pay.' It was chilling." The conspiracists say that Mayer made good on his threat by sabotaging the sound booth during the making of *His Glorious Night*. Metro's chief recording engineer, Douglas Shearer (Norma's brother and Irving Thalberg's brother-in-law), denied the story, but in the film, Gilbert, a stage-trained actor whose speaking voice had never struck anyone as inadequate, sounds like tin. James Card, the former director of Eastman House, suggests that the problem with *His Glorious Night* wasn't the sound of Gilbert's voice, but the awful writing, which was as purple as the subtitles in a silent melodrama. Take Gilbert's first, panting lines: "Oh, beauteous maiden, my arms are waiting to enfold you. Darling, I love you, I love you, I love you." After a few more awful roles, including one that Garbo hoped would rescue his career in 1933's *Queen Christina*, Gilbert died, ruined at forty-one.

Her no-show at the Boardman-Vidor wedding was the second humiliation and heartbreak Garbo caused Gilbert, if it can be believed that she had abandoned him a few months earlier on their way to a quick marriage somewhere in the desert. The gossip was that Garbo bolted off the train at a station stop, hid in the ladies' room, then scrambled out the window and hopped on the next train back to Los Angeles.

*I* hate speaking with accents. You think it's amusing. Well, it's probably amusing to Americans, but I happen not to like accents in any language. I don't think it's charming, I don't think it's cute, I don't think it's anything. It's silly. I prefer to speak the language without accents. I personally prefer to talk it the way it should be talked. I would never cultivate an accent.

By the end of 1929 the suspense was building, among the public, within the industry, and within Garbo herself: Would the microphone enhance her career or end it? Of the major players, only she, Lon Chaney, and Charles Chaplin had remained silent. The defiant Chaplin did not speak until *The Great Dictator* in 1940; Chaney died soon after filming his only talking picture, the 1930 remake of *The Unholy Three*. Metro had kept its top money-making actress mute, hoping, perhaps, for last-minute technological breakthroughs—an improvement on the Vitaphone system of synchronizing word and image, anything to give her an advantage in her transition to the new medium. But there could be no more stalling: Garbo would have to speak or stop making movies.

Eugene O'Neill's waterfront drama *Anna Christie* was Irving Thalberg's downbeat choice for Garbo's talking debut. She didn't much like the play, which had been filmed by D. W. Griffith in 1923, with Blanche Sweet as Anna, the broken, man-hating prostitute. (Sweet claimed that it actually was Garbo who suggested *Anna Christie,* but only after learning that the studio had offered Sweet the chance to remake it in sound. And of course Garbo got what Garbo wanted: The moment she expressed interest, Sweet was dropped from consideration.) Garbo trusted Thalberg's judgment about a role that would mark a departure in her repertoire of cosmopolitan heartbreakers and bejeweled divas.

Anna Christie is a difficult part, and a talky one, with monologues and wry verbal exchanges with other characters. In the Frances Marion treatment, O'Neill's heroine is "a tall, blond, fully developed girl of twenty, handsome ... but now run down in health and plainly showing all the outward evidences of belonging to the world's oldest profession." A Swedish immigrant abandoned as a child and raised in the Midwest, Anna seeks out her father (George F. Marion), who is living on a coal barge docked at New York's Battery, and redeems her life through a sailor she saves from drowning.

Though the setting is drab and the costumes are as subdued as the love scenes between Garbo and Charles Bickford, the story had a specific asset for the star: a character who spoke with a Swedish accent. If, as Metro feared, audiences would think that Garbo talked funny—well, she was supposed to. For *Anna Christie* Garbo had to master a particular manner of immigrant speech, and the irony of the matter did not escape her. "Here I've been learning English and now I have to practice a Swedish dialect," she said to Marie Dressler, who was cast as the saloon rat Marthy. During the making of the film, according to an item in the *Los Angeles Herald-Examiner*, Garbo had so "improved her English [that] she speaks with almost no accent. But, on the other hand, there are days when she lapses into Swedish and can scarcely be understood at all." Neither statement was true: Garbo always spoke with an accent, and she spoke Swedish only when she meant to.

For the director, Garbo summoned her most reliable, Clarence Brown, also one of the last professionals in Hollywood to leap into what he called "dialogue pictures." Brown had always maintained that people "absorb entertainment" more through the eyes than through the ears. "The essential of a motion picture is motion," he said, "and the less you rely on a flock of subtitles or pages of dialogue to explain your actions, the better." Brown considered his only other talking picture, *Navy Blues,* a warm-up for this historic moment with Garbo.

*Anna Christie* was like any other film for Garbo only in the almost grave professionalism she brought to the task. Arriving on the set for the first day's shooting, she announced, "I have learned my lines, Mr. Brown. I am ready to rehearse." She was anxious during filming; to Wilhelm Sorensen, her house guest at the time, she admitted feeling "like an unborn child." The studio's daily production reports suggest that the stress took its toll: She who had never before missed a day's work was sent home twice with an unspecified ailment. Garbo did not feel confident about most of her performance ("Whoever saw Swedes act like that?" she said to friends at an early screening), but she did like her scenes with the dramatically unglamorous Marie Dressler.

The premiere was set for March 14, 1930, "a real red-letter day," according to Hearst's *New York American.* With characteristic hyperbole *Variety* predicted "tidal waves" of fans at theaters across the country as MGM unfurled its two-word flag, one of advertising's immortal slogans: "Garbo Talks." Her vulgar first words in the movie added to the shock and thrill of hearing her speak: "Gimme a whiskey, ginger ale on the side. . . . And don't be stingy, baby." After tossing back the drink, she says, "Gee, I needed that bad alright, alright."

If, before, nothing like her had ever been seen on the screen, no one sounded like Garbo, either. The voice was called husky, contralto, profundo, wine-dark, and throaty. Was it more like velvet than silk, a cello or a viola, mahogany or ebony? It was definitely erotic, and had it been acceptable to have done so, it would have been labeled "bedroom." Lost in an aural spell, reviewers hardly referred to O'Neill's Pulitzer Prize winner. The *New York Times*'s Mordaunt Hall dwelled on Garbo's "surprisingly low intonations. . . . Whether she is dealing with straight English or the vernacular, she compels attention by her deep-toned enunciation and the facility with which she handles Anna's slang." Garbo sounded so unusual that some suspected technical foolery: Surely engineers at the studio or in projection rooms had exaggerated its depth and richness. As the picture played on, breaking twelve-week records at Loew's State theaters, everyone weighed in with an opinion or a crack about the siren and her spoken song: Anita

To check sound continuity, directors sometimes ran film backwards through a projector, creating a noise, according to Clarence Brown, "like nothing on earth." Garbo loved it. Brown recalled her "sitting there, shaking with laughter," watching the film [with] the sound going *yakablom-yakablom.*" As soon as Brown started to run the film forward, Garbo would go off to regain her composure for the next scene.

*Audiences could hear*
*a pin drop when*
*Garbo stepped into the*
*first scene of* Anna
Christie.

Loos likened her, or it, to "a Swedish foghorn" and director Fred
Niblo called Garbo "a blond with a brunette voice." Tallulah
Bankhead, no lightweight in the larynx department, felt bested:
She was no longer the only leading lady with a smoky chimney
for a throat.

*The star tarted up a bit for the German edition of the film.*

I never studied German, but I picked it up. I have a very small vocabulary in German. I wish I could speak German better than I do. Certain words are close to Swedish, but that doesn't make up the language. I never learned anything, just drifted along. Well, *Ganze Leben ist ein Schwindel* [All of life is a fraud].

Shortly after finishing *Anna Christie,* Garbo headed a new cast for a German version of the movie, directed by Jacques Feyder. (The star's enormous overseas following made her talking debut so commercially significant that Metro took the unusual step of reshooting it in a second language.) More at home in the German language, even making some improvements in the translation of the screenplay—and wearing different costumes—Garbo liked her performance this time around, as *Fräulein* Christie. At her request the role of Marthy was given to her friend Salka Viertel, the Polish actress and screenwriter. "She was always joking about her inadequate German and English," Viertel would later recall of Garbo. "But she expressed herself very well."

Though the praise for her talking debut was extravagant, hearing Garbo wasn't to everyone's liking. "We want our Garbo back," wrote one fan, "and the only way to get her . . . is in another silent film." Though Garbo would never be confused with the effusive girl next door, as she spoke she did sacrifice some of her mystery; and by making audible the sighs and whispered passions audiences had only imagined, she emerged as a mortal woman, somehow more attainable than before. In life, she remained silent as stone. But on screen, the sphinx finally had spoken.

Preceding page: *The invincible team of Garbo and Adrian.*

Are You the Garbo Type? Then Shun Makeup for the Street, Go Light on Jewels... Wear Black, White and Gray.

—FASHION ITEM, JUNE 25, 1930

*I*t's spring, shucks. In two days I'll be through with the closets. That's what I'm doing these days—cleaning out my closets, endlessly. There are *sacks* of clothes, *boxes, drawers* full of stuff. It's a project, it's horrible. I'm going to give it all away. The more you have, the less you have.

There are clothes in my closet that are fifty years old. I wear the same old things. Some days around here, you've never seen anything like it—I'm in my long underwear. I go in and out of the kitchen and say to my girl, "In case you're wondering, just pretend that I've joined the circus."

Garbo's fondness for sensible-to-a-fault street attire disillusioned her fans and put the glamour-press hounds in a snit, but she had the confidence to fall from couture grace. After all, her influence on fashion had been profound, not only on the styles of her moviemaking heyday but for all time. Watch her pace back and forth across a terrace in *The Single Standard:* The long, hurried stride is still mimicked on the fashion runway. As Parker Tyler pointed out, Garbo was the first to strike what became the model's insolent hand-on-hip pose and indifferent gaze—the "debutante slouch." "She invented so much that [became] fashion," wrote Cecil Beaton. "It's hard to remember all her originality."

Long before she met Valentina Schlee, who began dressing Garbo in the late 1940s, the star lived the imperious designer's credo of "Fit the century, forget the year." But Garbo transcended even centuries: As Arden Stuart, the Cosmo Girl of 1929's *The*

*Single Standard,* or as Christina, the seventeenth-century queen of Sweden who passed for a boy, she projected timeless appeal. In most of her silent pictures today, Garbo is uncannily contemporary, standing apart from the dated plots and from her fellow players. Tailored and slender, she was immortally modern, setting an all-time standard for fashionable young women whose schoolgirl crushes on her defined a national idolatry: Garbomania. "I remember how she looked in *The Single Standard,*" said George Cukor a half-century after the release of that film. "Every college girl looks that way today. . . . She's influenced the thinking of the world."

After walking through a department store one day in 1929, the film critic Robert E. Sherwood devoted a column in the humor magazine *Life* to the Garbo vogue: "Now [young women] are drooping their eyelids, thrusting their heads back and their shoulders forward, training their lengthening hair to fall all over on one side and to curl slightly at the ends; they are whitening their faces in simulation of interesting anemia; they are looking out at the world through the eye of disillusionment; they are doing a great deal of silent smoldering." Almost thirty-five years later, a spread in Time Inc.'s *Life,* called "Good Grief—It's Garbo!" celebrated the return of the Garbo Look among coeds and young career women.

*I* have the latest edition of *Vogue.* But I never read it properly—I look at it and let it go at that. I buy these magazines and then I give them to the girl who comes on Saturday. Most of the time I don't even remember having seen them.

Requisite to the Look was a cool demeanor, which, through heavy lids, simultaneously issued an invitation (come hither) and a warning (not too close). *Garboesque:* to look as Garbo looked (gorgeous, tired), to feel as she felt (tired, sad in love, ho-hum); to do as she did (sigh, suffer, seek solitude). *Garboesque:* to be marked by fate; to be secretive and aloof. When MGM launched an international search for a Garbo look-alike in 1932, thousands of young women drifted past panels of judges in Europe and the United States, all of the candidates striving to look bored beneath their hat brims.

> **Mary Anita Loos recalls an urgent afternoon call from her aunt, the writer Anita Loos, who whispered into the telephone, "Quick, Garbo's here ... Pretend you're out walking the dog and drop by." That is how the younger Loos met Garbo, who, she says, "couldn't have been more *fun*. She was wearing knickers, and a peanut-vendor hat —one of the straw ones. She asked me what I wanted to be when I grew up. Either an actress or an archaeologist, I said, but told her that I worried that I was too tall to be an actress. Well, she jumped up and said, 'Why just look at me—I'm an actress and I'm taller than you are,' and she grabbed a book to mark our heights against the wall. It was such a sweet thing to do."**

The fast evolution from gawky girl into goddess was the almost magical achievement of Mauritz Stiller and Garbo, as if they had willed the transformation in her. By the time she arrived at the studio all that was left to do was pluck and pencil her eyebrows into high arches—almost antennae—and cap her two front teeth, which protruded slightly. ("Her teeth are perfect—a dentist never touched them," a 1938 Metro press release fibbed.) But this newcomer was nothing at all like the current squeeze-doll darlings of the box office—Garbo didn't have the jazz-babiness of redhead Clara Bow, the blond punch of Mae Murray, or the bee-stung lips of either. Nor was she a cute, Dutch-boy tease like Colleen Moore. Casting directors whispered that she had a chest like a boy's, legs like tree trunks, and manly wrists and hands.

They said she was too indelicate for most leading men.

Feeling freakish was nothing new to Garbo. "Everywhere I went as a child I was pointed at because I was so big, so very big," she told a reporter soon after arriving in Hollywood. "I was just the same size I am now when I was twelve years old." But when she peered into a whirring MGM camera for the first time, her grace registered completely, and in a way it hadn't in the flesh, or in her European films, or even in the Arnold Genthe portraits. And her angular beauty knocked the more voluptuous kind off its pedestal.

Of course, not everyone would be captivated—or some said they weren't, anyway. Clare Boothe Luce slammed Garbo in *Vanity Fair* with a heavily hyphenated putdown, calling her "broad-shouldered, flat-chested, long-legged, raw-boned"—but then Luce also predicted that Garbo would "be forgotten as a woman [and] as an actress." But as shopgirls, secretaries, and coeds continued to worship their idol—and to buy multiple tickets to her movies—the studios began to frantically search for more Garbos, big-money answers to the Swedish Sensation.

Irving Thalberg was certain that Garbo lightning would strike again for MGM with Eva von Pletzner, a dancer he discovered in Vienna, brought to Hollywood, and renamed von Berne. Whatever had impressed Thalberg on the Viennese stage was not present in von Berne's starring performance opposite John Gilbert in 1928's *Masks of the Devil,* and Eva was sent home. Paramount succeeded with Marlene Dietrich, "the German Garbo," who had the architectural eyebrows and Arctic attitude to go with the title. Dietrich was Dietrich—very much herself and governed well (by Josef von Sternberg, who would achieve what had eluded Mauritz Stiller in Hollywood). But there were many other "new Garbos," some of them true and talented beauties:

- Elissa Landi, the "Empress of Emotion," whose imperial billing was legitimate (she was the granddaughter of Elizabeth of Austria);

- Vienna's Tala Birell, whose career slid from 1935's fine *Crime and Punishment* to the low-budget *Women in Bondage* of 1944;

■ "Goldwyn's folly," the squat, half-Swedish Anna Sten, recruited from Russian cinema in 1934 to star in Goldwyn's dismal production of Zola's *Nana;*

■ The Hungarian Zita Johann, Boris Karloff's love interest in *The Mummy;*

■ Gwili Andred, an Edward Steichen model from Denmark;

■ Sigrid Gurie, a "Norwegian beauty" from Brooklyn;

■ Germany's Dorothea Wieck, the headmistress in the lesbian drama *Mädchen in Uniform.*

Metro used two doubles for Garbo, Chris Marie Meeker and Geraldine De Vorak, whose duties included standing in for wardrobe fittings, lighting checks, and extreme long shots. De Vorak's resemblance to the star was particularly striking and she seems to have taken her job much too seriously, appearing on the street as Garbo, signing autographs, living her life as the star. "She is," wrote one Hollywood reporter apparently frustrated over the unavailability of the real thing, "what Garbo should be and isn't."

When a twenty-six-film Garbo festival opened at New York's Museum of Modern Art in the summer of 1968, *Vogue* published its own fashion retrospective for the benefit of the innocents who were encountering the actress for the first time—they were, in the magazine's phrase, "the Generation That Never Knew." *Women's Wear Daily* joined in the celebration, telling the uninitiated that the whole concept of fashion freedom—why, modern art itself—began with Garbo.

*I* 've had terrible nights lately—something went wrong, something that I ordered to wear. That's why I'm trekking down today, for a fitting. I stood for an hour and a half and I really was ready to fold up. I was shaking. But he said, "I didn't know you had such patience." You try on canvas things, you see, for fit. The man said, "Could you possibly come back on Friday?" They wanted to make another canvas, and I just have to come again. If I don't it can go wrong again and in the end it's too hard on one. If you get the *wrong* things you have nothing anyway.

They should know what they're doing, but there's no good craftsmanship today. They don't quite know . . . they can do for the masses, on the racks, but they can't do individual things very easily because that requires a really good craftsmanship. They don't have it today. Today, everything is sloppy. They can't even build ships anymore. Nobody cares.

I'll never go to sleep now.

No one looked more at ease in finery than Garbo—every designer wanted to drape her—but no star felt more encumbered by clothes than she. At the studio, relief came at the stroke of five p.m., when she could throw off her costumes and pull on her well-worn trousers and sweaters. Garbo dreaded fittings almost from the beginning of her career. "More than twenty costumes to try on, over and over," she said to a reporter while making *The Temptress.* "That is why I do not care about clothes. There are so many clothes in every picture. I cannot think of them when I am away from work."

But she was no fool about the importance of looking exactly right before the camera, and from the very beginning of her professional life had complied with the demands of such perfection: This, after all, was the girl who so eagerly modeled hats for a department-store catalog and, as the baggy-pants buffoon in the short "How Not to Dress," displayed innate fashion sense—and immense pleasure—in wrapping herself in woolens and silks. The Empire-style gowns of *The Saga of Gösta Berling* suit her splendidly, and her longing for a fur coat in *Joyless Street* is almost erotic.

*T*hat's a magic world, couture. The designers rule the world. It's fantastic when you think of it. Chanel had a fabulous life. She lived in great luxury, houses and things, jewels. That ugly woman—she looked like a monkey, but very striking.

At first Metro blundered in its costuming of Garbo, forcing her into plunging necklines and obscuring her with lace, feathers, and fur. In her early films she managed to tame some of the

*Before Adrian: Lost in a cocoon; opposite, spreading clumsy wings.*

wildest ensembles (a number of them designed by a fellow Scandinavian, the Danish Max Ree): a sequined, stand-up cape in *The Torrent;* an off-the-shoulder sheath that fits her like a bandage in *The Mysterious Lady;* diaphanous skirts in *The Divine Woman.* Her rescue arrived in 1929, when Adrian was assigned to do the costumes for *A Woman of Affairs.* Born Adrian Adolph Greenberg, this son of Connecticut milliners trained in the MGM costume department and became its chief designer, whipping up queenly robes for Norma Shearer and satin skins for Jean Harlow. But the studio's biggest star inspired his finest work. It was a remarkable partnership, Adrian's clothes and Garbo's ability to wear them, and an added attraction now preceded each of her films: What fabulous things would she be wearing this time?

"Simplicity is Garbo's god," declared Adrian, who liberated her from frills. "Not only does she live by it, but she responds to it in others." As his inspiration in dressing her Adrian cited Swe-

Greta
GARBO
AS
Mata Hari
TEMPTRESS OF THE SECRET SERVICE
Co-starring Ramon
NOVARRO
A Metro-Goldwyn-Mayer PICTURE

den: "an elemental, raw country, of iron and tallow . . . where one is close to the soil," speaking as if he would mine a new woman from that bedrock. His basic look for Garbo was modest and dignified, in medium to high necklines and long sleeves, with a minimum of prints, patterns, and ornamentation.

But because she made it possible for him to do so, Adrian also could break his rules for Garbo, and his designs for her period films of the 1930s, especially the ball gowns of *Romance* and *Camille,* define silk-and-satin excess. "The most interesting thing about her was her ability to wear a thing and create a style with a complete [lack of] self-consciousness," he said. "No matter how eccentric a thing was, Garbo wore it with confidence, and gave it an air of authority." Adrian could be severe with his geometries —this is the man who padded Joan Crawford's shoulders—and his black cabaret dress for Garbo in *As You Desire Me* is almost constructivist. The spangled, torso-revealing temple gown of *Mata Hari* is a precursor of Bob Mackie's creations for Cher.

Adrian's costumes—assembled in Metro's spare-no-expense wardrobe department— are prizes at auction: In 1989, a pleated and caped velvet dress from *Queen Christina* sold for $9,500. Collectors have paid more than $3,000 for individual sketches.

Elements of Adrian's designs for Garbo, even those for her most extravagant costume dramas, were successfully adapted to ladies' apparel. The feathered hat she wore cocked over one eye in *Romance* "turned the heads of all the girls into Empress Eugenies," noted one fashion writer. Even the epaulet jackets of *Queen Christina* came into vogue. When the "Greta Garbo Skirt," a knock-off of a black jumper from *Susan Lenox,* hit department-store racks, Macy's ads claimed that "every girl who sees it insists on having one."

Garbo got a kick out of sporting turtlenecks at a time when only jockeys and prizefighters wore them, and she was the first film star, followed by Katharine Hepburn and Marlene Dietrich,

One of Garbo's favorite garments was a skirted Paul Poiret coat that she had admired on Mercedes de Acosta, who drew stares in it—and a zinger from Tallulah Bankhead, who described her as "a mouse in a topcoat." But when Garbo was photographed in it, de Acosta predicted that the coat would be the next rage. "Last year I was démodé," she wrote, "but soon, no doubt, I will be in fashion. . . ."

to liberate women from skirts. Knowing observers slipped innuendo into their reports of Garbo and Dietrich's preference for masculine styles. *Vanity Fair* pictured the Swede and the German, in 1932, under the headline "Both Members of the Same Club," implying more than their mutual fondness for men's suits and slouch hats.

Women who spurned skirts were not only violating taboos at the time, but breaking laws; in Paris in the twenties, a *permis de travestissement* was required of any female wearing a man's suit. Mores were not much more relaxed on Hollywood Boulevard. "Garbo in Pants!" shouted a wire-photo caption. "Innocent bystanders gasped in amazement to see Mercedes de Acosta and

Garbo in pants pretty much managed to go where she pleased (and, perversely, she didn't seem to mind the extra attention her fashion preferences brought her). One night in 1978 Bill Frye slipped her into Chasen's by rolling her trousers up beneath her overcoat, which she wore to the table. "We had already booked the reservation," says Frye, "and when I saw what she was wearing I called the restaurant and told them I was bringing Miss Garbo to dinner and could she please come in slacks. They said no, she could not. I asked, 'What if you put us to the right, just as we come in the door?' They still said no, so we played our little trick."

*Garbo as she appeared in* Vanity Fair, *"making the world safe for the slouch hat."*

Garbo dismissed one of Cecil Beaton's marriage proposals b telling him, "You wouldn't like to see me in the morning in an old man's pajamas."

Greta Garbo striding swiftly along . . . dressed in men's clothes."
A few days later, MGM sent out a story under Garbo's name, in
which she apologized for inflicting her "trousered attitude" on
hostesses, escorts, and maîtres d'.

*I* would've gotten wet, totally soaked—I was out today in
the rain without an umbrella. But I was wearing a hat. I
always do and always did. I wear hats all the time, but I do
it because I have to cover the hair.

For the street Garbo liked coolie hats and anything with a
wide brim, under which she could hide; but she also liked toques,
and she made berets permanently fashionable. She was so devoted to the slouch hat that it is forever known as the "Garbo."

Her hair was a dark blond, the color of the camomile tea in
which she rinsed it. Garbo at first was not choosy about who did
her hair at Metro, and relied on staff stylists who worked from

photographs and sketches. But when Sydney Guilaroff arrived at the studio in 1935, he became her exclusive hairdresser. Though Garbo is done up in ringlets in *Camille* and wears a bleached-blond wig in the opening scenes of *As You Desire Me,* Guilaroff's signature coiffures for her were not at all fussy. Cropped below the chin, the long "Garbo bob" was widely copied, and when she tried something different, such as cutting her hair in bangs for *Susan Lenox,* so did many of her fans. "No statistician could compute the number of feminine heads in the world that in the last five years have been coiffed in slavish imitation of Garbo's," ran a 1933 column in *Vogue.* "Longish, blond, straight, and lanky on top and on the sides, and curled up on the ends—such a hairdress was never seen in Paris or anywhere else before the advent of the Swedish Miracle."

As the adulterous Irene Guarry in her last silent picture, 1929's *The Kiss,* Garbo wears her hair up, and Metro's daily production reports suggest some concern over the matter (and prove that Garbo did look at rushes when she had to):

*Three more of her many hats.*

After returning from Italy in October of 1938, Garbo was censured for her hairdo. In a joint proclamation the International Master Ladies' Hairdressers Association and the Coiffure Guild of New York criticized her untidy cut and long bangs as "wholly unsuited for wear by her or by the women of this country." At the moment the two professional groups were advocating "upswept" hairstyles, which required the permanent waves and regular maintenance° that kept beauty operators in business.

Inspired by Italian television's 1963 "Festivale di Garbo," Rome hairdresser Alberto Francesca unveiled a modified pageboy, "il G.G." The week-long series of broadcasts broke the national network's viewing records—only Anna Magnani movies had kept more millions of Italians at home—and Francesca did a brisk business with "the G.G."

*After her impromptu 1938 press conference, Garbo was scolded for her "unsuitable" haircut.*

July 18: "Miss Garbo in projection room looking at rushes to determine change in her hairdress."

August 14: "Miss Garbo fixing hair, 9:40 a.m.–9:50."

August 19: "Miss Garbo not on set until 9:50 after discussing with Mr. Feyder [Jacques Feyder, the director] decision to change her hairdress. Changing hairdress until 10:10."

*H*air gets in the way most times. You can hide behind it or under it, but I prefer just not to fool with it.

When Edward Steichen came to photograph her, Garbo was on the set of *The Mysterious Lady* and gave him only a few minutes between scenes, covering her costume with a black shawl. Steichen didn't like the way her curls fell down around her face, saying, "It's too bad we're doing this with that movie hairdo." Said Garbo, "Oh, that terrible *hair,*" and obliged him by covering it almost completely with her hands. Steichen captured Garbo as Clarence Bull never could when he photographed her in character and costume: A reflective, brooding woman—seeming far more mature than her twenty-four years—stares out from what is probably the best known and arguably the most beautiful photograph ever taken of her. In another of the nine pictures from the six-minute session, Garbo's hair is prominent, a mane falling to one side as she glares to her right, toward someone who has called her back to the set. Though she never arranged another, less hurried, sitting with Steichen, Garbo apparently had enjoyed this one. "You understand me," she told him. "You should direct motion pictures." Afterward, Steichen described Garbo as "a lovely wild-wood animal."

*I* was up at Saks today, to see Mrs. Cole's swimsuits and things. I tried on some, and the girls there made such a fuss over me. Oh, it was very nice, very sweet. They let me take

*A last-minute fix for the final scene of* Conquest.

things home, so I can decide if I want to keep them. I saw a suit, black silk, and the girl—eighteen or twenty years old—put it on for me. I could never get into it because I don't have the body for it. But they're youngsters.

You want to go shopping with me? Why? Shopping is not fun. I never liked to shop. Men have it so easy, it's so easy for men to shop—and so it's easy for them to pack. That's half the difficulty of traveling—having to figure out what to buy, and what to pack. It takes me weeks. Who can sort it all out, what to buy, what to take along?

Paralyzed by the idea of assembling a travel wardrobe for her trip home to Sweden in 1932, Garbo called on her friend Lilyan Tashman, sophisticate of the silent screen and one of the best-dressed women in Hollywood. Tashman accompanied Garbo on a shopping expedition to New York, and whenever Garbo spotted something she liked, she nudged Tashman and said, *"That* is going back to Sweden!" Years later, her affirmative had become the less enthusiastic, "I wouldn't throw it back."

Dorothy Kilgallen had been filing Garbo sightings for ten years—Garbo toting hatboxes, Garbo in cashmere, Garbo alligator-belted—when she wrote in her *New York Post* column on April 20, 1959: "Fans who believe the legend that the Great One never wears anything but a slouch hat and a beat-up raincoat should have seen her casing the French and Italian fashions at Saks the other day. Greta wound up buying three coats: a white faille by Balenciaga, a black taffeta Lanvin Castillo wrap, and Monsieur X's glamorous black satin trench coat."

Escorting Billy Baldwin through her East Fifty-second Street apartment, Garbo led the decorator into a room lined on three sides by closets, which she opened to reveal racks of dresses, hundreds of them. "Master Billy," she said, "I have never worn a single one."

When Garbo needed to outfit her new life after Hollywood, her friend the nutritionist Gayelord Hauser and his publicist, Eleanor Lambert, took control, delivering her to Valentina Schlee's salon in the Sherry-Netherland Hotel. "She really had no interest in fashion then," says Lambert. "But she blossomed with Valentina. When the right people dressed Garbo, the results were absolutely perfect. She was like an armature for clothes." It was a fateful day for Garbo, marking her introduction to George Schlee, the designer's husband and business manager. As Lambert remembers it, Garbo was shown to a downstairs fitting room. After a few moments George went to check on her and found Garbo stark naked, standing on a pedestal, surrounded by walls of mirrors. "That was just the way she was," says Lambert. "She was Swedish, and she was an actress. She would take off her clothes to try on a hat."

Valentina called herself "an architect of clothes," and her enigmatic and extravagant pronouncements about nothing ("Mink is for football, ermine is for bathrobes") would rival Diana Vreeland's and make her the Marie Antoinette of her day. She had begun her career in the theater (she designed Katharine Hepburn's costumes for the stage production of *The Philadelphia Story*) and her retail enterprise catered to her own international, well-heeled crowd. The clothes were practical, though—as timeless as togas, someone said—and Garbo liked the collection enormously. In linen, cashmere, and cotton, Valentina's separates would, for a while anyway, spare Garbo the agony of deciding what to wear and what to pack. There were free-flowing skirts of various lengths, jackets and trousers, tunics, and capes, all unencumbered by surface pattern or print. Colors were limited to off white and ivory, beige, navy blue, charcoal, and black. There were ballet slippers for the feet; turbans, coolie hats, and babushkas for the head.

It would follow that Halston's clean line and subdued palette, which echoed Valentina's, would suit Garbo, and one afternoon in 1977 her friend Sam Green escorted her to the designer's atelier on Fifth Avenue. Garbo agreed that the clothes were just right, and indicated that she would return for fittings. But when an item appeared in the next day's newspapers about Halston's coup—that is, snaring Garbo as a customer—she backed out.

Valentina died at the age of ninety-one, in September of 1989, and her estate contained a few items from her closet which sold well at Christie's: linen blouses, $660; a beige voile dress, $3,740; a beige, hooded cape made of crepe, $3,520. Her coolie hats brought more than $100 each.

*I* have more shoes on my shelves than anybody living, and I have to give them away. I can't find any shoes, you see. I buy these dancing shoes, those soft ones, size 8B. I can't find any other shoes that will go on me. I can't go into a shop and say, "Give me a size 8 or size 9," because it doesn't fit. Nothing fits. I've tried everything. What am I supposed to do? It's so sad.

The rumor that Garbo had large feet apparently was started by Antonio Moreno, her co-star in *The Temptress*, who claimed that he had to wear shoes two sizes too large to make hers seem smaller. She encouraged such stories by wearing men's oxfords, which went so well with her manly ensembles of trousers, shirts and ties, vests, and overcoats. Buying four or five pair at a time, Garbo would try them on and say to anyone present, "Just the thing for us bachelors, eh?"

A newswire from Florence, Italy, dated October 1950 confirmed that the fetish about Garbo's feet was worldwide and had not abated almost ten years after she left Hollywood: "The secret is out. Greta Garbo wears a size 7AA shoe. Salvatore Ferragamo, the world-famous Florentine shoemaker, offered this information after Miss Garbo ordered seventy pairs of his renowned handmade shoes during her two-day visit." Said Ferragamo, "Seldom have I found among my clientele a person with such well-proportioned feet."

The only quarrels Adrian ever had with Garbo were about her feet. "She always wanted her gowns just escaping the floor," said the designer. "Her feet kept coming out. I didn't think it was pretty." Garbo often worked in flats or even bedroom slippers, shunning Adrian's pumps whenever she could. Just before the cameras rolled, Garbo would call out to the crew, half-jokingly,

"Is the feets in?" The line was mimicked around town, and Garbo's feet became as funny as Durante's nose. Which was bigger—Garbo's feet or her salary? Then there was the one, supposedly told by Garbo herself, about the manager of a shoe store in Los Angeles who saw the star approaching and brought out boxes of size 9s and 10s for her to try on. Seeing that her feet were swallowed by the shoes, he said, "Excuse me, ma'am, I thought you were Miss Garbo." Many years later in New York, Garbo did not laugh when she spotted a sign in I. Miller's window on Fifth Avenue. "We Can Fit Anybody's Feet," it read. "Even Garbo's." Her feelings were hurt, and she took the unusual step of instructing her lawyer, Eustace Seligman, to ask that the sign be removed. It was.

In "Hollywood Steps Out," a 1941 Warner Bros. cartoon set at the Mocambo nightclub, Garbo, in ski-size sandals, gets a hot foot from Harpo Marx. As the matches flare up between her giant toes, she utters a cool, four-syllable "Ouch."

Though Garbo could be caricatured—droopy eyelids, a pouty lower lip, whopping feet—she never inspired a brilliant drag act. Her kind of femininity gave impersonators too little to play off—drag simply cannot derive from androgyny. ("She is really hermaphroditic, with the cold quality of a mermaid," said Tennessee Williams, describing his first encounter with Garbo.) Perhaps Garbo's features were too perfect to exaggerate, her image too humorless. (Even Charles Ludlam, tossing ringlets in his production of *Camille*, had more fun with the Dumas book than with Garbo's incarnation of the heroine.)

129

*In* Mother Goose Goes Hollywood, *a 1939 Disney cartoon by T. Hee, Garbo, perched on a seesaw opposite Edward G. Robinson, purrs the line forever attributed to her, "I want to be alone."*

THE
LOOK

Eleanor Boardman, one of the few actresses at MGM who got to know Garbo outside the studio, says that the star was forever in need of something decent to wear, especially shoes. "She hated to shop," says Boardman. "She wasn't interested in spending money. She wouldn't have had anything to wear if friends hadn't taken her shopping."

Boardman recalls an afternoon expedition with Garbo:

"She wanted new shoes. *Needed* them. There were no stores in Beverly Hills then, you had to go to Los Angeles, so I had the driver take us to Gude's, a shoe store downtown. Garbo found a pair she liked, just one, paid for them, and walked out with them on her feet. We did a lot that day— some more shopping and we had lunch somewhere. Later on Garbo said, 'They *hurt* my feet. I take them back.'

" 'G.G.,' I said, 'you can't take them back— you've worn them all day.'

" 'They *hurt*. I take them back. Tell the driver.'

" 'You can't do that.'

" 'Yes, I must.'

"So of course, we took them back. I was so embarrassed, but the man in the store was lovely about it."

After George Schlee died in 1964, Garbo increasingly took to drab uniforms and dark glasses. She may have thought that by dressing down she was disguising herself, but she was not. "Greta Garbo walks the East Side of New York undisguised," wrote Dorothy Kilgallen in 1965, "in her sensible, social-worker shoes, old trenchcoat, and slouch hat."

But if she looked awful, so what? Who could hurt her? In 1982 Garbo showed up at a Los Angeles dinner party wearing "a terrible little polyester pants suit," according to *Vogue*'s Eleanor Phillips Colt. "Her hair was tied back with this little rubber band, and she was wearing the kind of shoes you'd buy in a notions department. Well, Gayelord [Hauser], who always told Garbo how to dress, said, 'Oh, G.G., how can you dress like that when a fashion editor is here?' And she said to him, 'No one will attack *me.*' She knew who she was. It wasn't offensive, what she had on, but it was amusing. She wore no makeup at all, none, and her hair was simply too long—stringy, really, but it didn't matter. The bones were all there, the bone structure was there. She always had the bones."

When Garbo first appeared on the American screen in *The Torrent,* reviewers were at a loss to describe her, and got little help from MGM publicists, who trotted her out as "the Norma Shearer of Sweden," then as a composite of Carol Dempster, Zasu Pitts, Norma Talmadge, and Gloria Swanson. The *New York Morning Telegraph* didn't zero in on her appeal, either, but it did herald

*In the arbor scene in Flesh and the Devil, William Daniels lit Garbo's face with a pen light, concealed in the cup of John Gilbert's hands. Daniels "understood her face and its potentials like an engineer knows a fine machine," wrote Bosley Crowther.*

*Going beautifully blank: Garbo in the last frames of* Queen Christina.

her as the possessor of "what is often said to be lacking in motion pictures, a new face." That face has been contemplated and caused rapture for most of the twentieth century. To Roland Barthes, the exchange that occurs in a darkened theater between the image of Garbo's face and its beholders became a kind of ritual:

> Garbo belongs to that moment in cinema when capturing the human face still plunged audiences into the deepest ecstasy, when one literally lost oneself in a human image . . . when the face represented a kind of absolute state of the flesh, which could be neither reached nor renounced. . . . Garbo offered to one's gaze a sort of Platonic Idea of the human creature, which explains why her face is almost sexually undefined, without however leaving one in doubt. It is . . . always the same snowy solitary face . . . descended from a heaven where all things

are formed and perfected in the clearest light ... not to have any reality except that of its perfection, which was intellectual even more than formal.

If Garbo's countenance is a vessel for those who look upon it —a clean canvas or blank page—then that is why the final frames of *Queen Christina,* as directed by Rouben Mamoulian, are so powerful. Playing Sweden's enigmatic Christina, Garbo has renounced her throne for a lover who has since been killed. In the last scene she sets sail for an unknown future. What is she feeling —sadness? anger? betrayal? Garbo asked Mamoulian what emotion she should register. "Nothing," said the director, instructing her to drain her face of feeling, to go blank. "Feel nothing ... [and] don't even blink your eyes. ... If you sob, some won't like it; if you smile, some won't like it. Sorrow or serenity, no actor could act the right thing. Let each man and woman write on your face." In the last moments of the film, Garbo stands at the prow of her ship, in extreme close-up. Her expression is not cold or stoic, but totally passive: She is giving herself over to us to complete.

The things that are striking about people are first of all their eyes and tone, those two things—their eyes and the sound of their voices. The way they move, too—you can judge a human being a lot by that. But mostly it's the eyes.

Garbo distinguished herself from other actors in the silent era whose gesticulations gave the term "silent opera" to the craft. Unlike some of her grimacing, eye-popping colleagues on screen, Garbo was a master of deep, subtle expressions. As Arnold Genthe had, the men in Hollywood who worked with Garbo most declared that her extraordinary power on film emanated from the eyes:

Clarence Brown: "She had something behind the eyes that you couldn't see until you photographed it in close-up. If she had to look at one person with jealousy, and another with love, she didn't have to change her expression. You could see it in her eyes. Nobody else has been able to do that on the screen."

Clarence Bull: "You could read her through her eyes. That's

why we made so many big pictures of her, to see what she was thinking."

William Daniels: "I didn't create a 'Garbo face,' but I always did try to make the camera peer into her eyes, to see what was there. She has the most beautiful eyes I ever saw."

Victor Seastrom: "She thinks above her eyes. Certain great actors possess what seems to be an uncanny ability to register thought—Lon Chaney was one, Garbo is another. They seem literally to absorb impressions. . . . Garbo is more sensitive to emotions than film is to light, [and] you see it through her eyes.

Diana Vreeland added to the testimonials in 1981, when Sam Green brought Garbo to tea at Vreeland's Park Avenue apartment. According to Green, Garbo was unusually animated that day, entertaining their hostess with chatter and by strutting around in the late Mr. Vreeland's cashmere coats. Diana Vreeland, for a change, was the audience, and back in her office at the Metropolitan Museum's Costume Institute, she gave an enthusiastic account of the afternoon to her assistant, Elaine Hunt. "If I could do what she can do with those eyes," said Vreeland, "why, I'd *be* Garbo."

*T*he faces you see on the street are really the way you think they're going to be—that people are being killed off by the air pollution. They all look absolutely pale and putty. I took out my mirror and said, "*You* look the same too?" And I had to answer, "Ya." Well, blame it on time—time, bloody old time.

"It isn't so good to get used to one's face," said Garbo, who even in her twenties rarely was known to primp, and all but banned mirrors from her Hollywood homes. Ernst Lubitsch, who directed Garbo in *Ninotchka*, found her to be the least vain of any actress, free of the "slavish devotion to the mirror. . . . She never looked at herself unless I told her to do so."

Clarence Bull said many times that Garbo was the most beautiful woman he ever photographed, yet also the least difficult and narcissistic, never fretting about her good or bad sides, or the way

Opposite: *Garbo was the modern incarnation of the Renaissance sculpture ideal of "vago": an expression of undefined vagueness, gracefulness, loveliness.*

he chose to light her. But she was precisely aware of every detail that transpired between them in his studio. Bull claimed that she could actually feel light and shadow—she could sense when the moment was right for him to click the shutter. Later, skimming through the ninety-odd proofs from a typical session, she immediately knew if any shots were missing. "There are two I don't see here," she might say. If she didn't like a particular picture, however, there was no huffing and puffing about it. "These," Garbo would say, "I hope you don't send out." (By the terms of her MGM contract, Garbo received a copy of all of Bull's prints. No one can say what has happened to that trove of some two thousand photographs.)

Even if she had been inclined to do so, Garbo had no exotic beauty secrets to share with fans who wanted to emulate her. Her real-life regimen was almost as simple as the one she uses as Queen Christina, running a handful of snow over her face. Garbo washed with castile soap and hot water, sometimes following the last rinse with ice chips. She gave herself facials at home, over a slowly steaming kettle. Believing salt crystals were good for her skin, she took nude plunges into the ocean. She sunbathed year-round, in the days before anyone knew about the leathering effects of ultraviolet radiation. On camera or not, her makeup consisted of a light foundation, sometimes followed by a quick brush of powder, but no rouge. She wore lipstick but called it "messy and degrading." Garbo did use eyeliner, shaded her eyelids, and brushed on mascara, sometimes heavily. (Cecil Beaton asked her why, and she replied, "Because I am an Oriental.") When *Photoplay* editor James Quirk accused her of having to wear false eyelashes "to put over her seductress routines," William Daniels spoke up for her, saying, "Garbo's eyelashes are the kind that don't come off," and Hedda Hopper assured fans that Garbo's eyelashes "literally sweep her cheeks." As Mata Hari, Garbo places the hands of her blinded lover (Ramon Navarro) over her eyes and delivers one of the coyest of all the self-referential lines ever written for her: "Here are your eyes, with those ridiculously long lashes, as you say."

In *Look Younger, Live Longer,* Gayelord Hauser detailed the "Garbo manner" of applying eye makeup: "Apply a bit of eye creme to the lid *immediately* above the roots of the lashes. Now draw a line with your crayon, working [it] between the lashes with short up-down strokes.... Now, with a clean finger, in the same motion clean the eyelid, leaving the penciling to adhere only to the roots of the lashes, which now look twice as thick, longer, and make your eyes seem larger, more opened and alert."

In the 1960s, Erno Laszlo revealed what he claimed to be one of his secret concoctions for Garbo, a "facial recipe" consisting of ground beef, egg, and milk. Allowed to dry on the skin, then rinsed off with lukewarm water, "it makes the skin glow," said Laszlo of the home remedy, which was to be used in conjunction with his own bottled (and costly) dermatological preparations.

*I*f I hadn't been in the movies and people didn't look you over too carefully, I could go places. I'd go anyplace at the drop of a hat. I've never wanted any kind of attention from anybody, except to know that someone likes me—that's nice. Otherwise, it's all so false.

I could never really travel, because I used to be in the movies. There are these horrible, unbelievable paparazzi. I think they hate humanity, these people. All they care about is "What does she look like today?" And look at me—the Madwoman of Chaillot, hair hanging.

I'm not in the movies many, many years. I'm not worth anything to anybody. Why do they harass me? Pick on people who are au courant. I've always wanted two lives—one for the movies, one for myself.

The week Garbo died, a eulogy that appeared on the editorial page of the *New York Times* proved, perhaps, that she had been right to hide from a world obsessed with age and beauty. "She was wise to quit when she did," stated the *Times*, "before time had started wearing at her face. The real Garbo could afford to grow old; the screen Garbo could not." She had, of course, learned that early in her career. "On the stage, you have your voice," said the theater-trained Garbo before there were talking pictures. "But in the movies, only your face." From the beginning, observers had dwelled on her looks. Her first critical notice, for *Peter the Tramp*, consisted of a caption in the Swedish magazine *Swing*, predicting that she "could become a Swedish film star." Why? Only because of "her Anglo-Saxon appearance." Even as she grew as an actress, her looks seemed to count more than her art. After Garbo left the movies, Rouben Mamoulian was asked if he thought she was happy. "That's the last word I would use to describe her," he answered. "Stars look at themselves and they see their beauty is gone, their youth is past. It's a tough experience, and much harder on actresses. Beauty has so much to do with their fame."

Garbo's final film, *Two-Faced Woman*, tampered with the most eloquent fashion statement ever to come out of Hollywood. In the mistaken-identity sex farce, she plays the double role of a nature-girl ski instructor and her giddy, nightclubby twin, a vamp who parodies the "old Garbo." Many on her trusted team blundered: the writers, led by Salka Viertel; the director, George Cukor; but especially Sydney Guilaroff and Adrian.

Metro publicists celebrated the new look. "The long Garbo bob, for years the symbol of glamour, is no more. Greta Garbo has had her hair cut short—which means . . . that the girls had better get out their scissors." The girls didn't, because this time no one cared to emulate Garbo. Adrian's designs were disastrous: low-cut, sleeveless dresses, a see-through nightgown, high-heeled bedroom pumps, and a two-piece, skirted bathing suit in which, *Life* opined, Garbo revealed "a boyish physique [that] would win no Miss America contests." (Katharine Hepburn says she did not, as others have told it, lend the bathing suit to Garbo, who was in a panic about having to do a swimming scene.) For once Garbo is not dazzling or at ease in Adrian's clothes; except in her skiing outfits, she looks embarrassed.

The movie caused a brief furor (the story virtually endorses adultery), then disappeared—and so did Garbo. Adrian followed her, leaving MGM with a pointed epitaph: "When the glamour ends for Garbo, it also ends for me." He eventually opened boutiques in New York and Beverly Hills, but in the era of Dior's relaxed New Look, his rather formal collections failed. For Adrian, there indeed was no glamour after Garbo.

When Garbo finally committed herself to a comeback film in 1948 —in Walter Wanger's production of *La Duchesse de Langeais*—it had been nearly ten years since she faced a camera. By then, "the greasepaint was a little thick," as William Daniels recalled Garbo's look, but he was also convinced that she "could still be photographed and be as beautiful as ever." Daniels was not available, however, to conduct her first and only color screen test, a task which fell to James Wong Howe, the cinematographer. Howe did not know Garbo well and had expected her to sweep into the studio with an entourage. She came alone and was simply dressed, in slacks, a white blouse, and a big black hat. Politely excusing herself, she slipped off to do her own hair and makeup, going easy on the rouge and powder. Forty-five minutes later, she was back on the set, which consisted of a garden table and a column. She asked for a cigarette and seemed distracted, but, according to Howe, "the minute the camera started rolling, she took on, oh . . . a wonderful emotional feeling . . . she expressed a wonderful emotional feeling of some kind, with a cigarette. It excited me. You [could] see this creature come alive." Howe lit Garbo every which way—from above, from behind, straight into her eyes. He illuminated the rising smoke from her cigarette. Nearly an hour later, she abruptly ended the test with a Garboism: "I think I go home."

Cecil Beaton found the same to be true when Garbo agreed to let him photograph her. Her excuse was that she needed a passport picture, but she obviously enjoyed the sitting. Most of the pictures would never do for a passport: There are haughty profiles, complete with cigarette holder, and Garbo being playful with a kitten, posing in rain hat and boots, reclining on a sofa. At forty-one, she had not faced a camera for five years and was what some might call a mature beauty—as an article in *Mirabella* pointed out, she looked a decade older than her age. Garbo was furious at Beaton when a few of the photographs appeared in *Vogue*. But what a dignified, intelligent presence! The Beaton portraits only prove that Garbo fled the screen much too soon.

**6 HER SELF**

Preceding page:
*Garbo contemplates*
*grapes in* Queen
Christina.

A fter my last siege I had a month of toast and some kind of tea, and the doctor said, "You can have some cream cheese with it." And I said, "Cream cheese? *Cream cheese?*" But doctors don't know anything about food. Nothing. They don't in hospitals, either.

The food I adore, probably it's helping make me sick, like those Australian apricots, awfully goody. Maison Glacé, also—you can get that at Gristede's. I wonder if they have *spraaten*—fish, like sardines. In cans. Terribly goody. I don't know where one gets them; I've forgotten where I used to get them.

I always buy fresh vegetables. They're everywhere, and it doesn't take brains to fix them. They don't taste like anything and they just sit there, you want to throw them out, but I'll tell you a little secret you can use: Buy sour cream. They sell it in buckets. All you do is take a great big heap of sour cream and put it on a vegetable with salt and it's delicious. No calories, calories, nay, no more than margarine. A big smack of it. It's simple and it's ready and it tastes good. It's more fun than with margarine. So get your sour cream and get going.

I'd adore to eat right now, but I can't. I happen to have a very peculiar stomach department. I haven't got enough things to digest food with. . . . If you don't have hydrochloric acid or whatever it is, then the stomach goes on strike. I don't know what the hell is wrong with me, I really don't, but down we are.

I can eat apples, but papaya's not very good for me. But you can't go by me because I don't have a normal stomach. No—I pay for everything I eat. If I had a normal stomach it would be marvelous. Very boring the whole thing.

Well, it's a waste of life, to invent things that are so goody but then we can't have them.

The world didn't revolve around what Garbo ate and how she stayed fit, not the way it did around how she looked, but her quirky diets and exercise regimens did generate a lot of wonder. Commanded by Mauritz Stiller and Louis B. Mayer to lose weight, she was a diet fanatic by the age of nineteen, and remained one all of her life. Like any food faddist, Garbo cooked up her own peculiar rules, alternately denying herself and indulging in an

*Metro introduced Garbo as a tomboy in a 1925 publicity campaign.*

array of edibles—beef one week, sweets the next, salt, citrus fruits, shellfish—compensating in idiosyncratic ways when she fell off of her various dietary wagons (though she never proscribed alcohol or tobacco or caffeine). A lifelong devotee of two nutrition gurus, Gayelord Hauser and Dr. Henry Bieler, Garbo nonetheless went culinarily wherever her cravings took her. A carnivorous vegetarian, she munched on roots pulled from the soil (on picnics, she actually *wore* carrots, hanging them in bunches from her belt) but she also made sure her meat came bloody. By the time she settled in New York, she might stock up on dried figs and whole milk at her East Side health-food stores in the morning, then turn up for lunch at the St. Regis for a rare steak and black coffee. When she at last got herself a real home, on East Fifty-second Street, she took pride in fending for herself in her small kitchen—she set an alarm clock for six o'clock some evenings, reminding her to start dinner.

Mine is a real bachelor's existence. Every day I have lunch on top of my bed, never anywhere else. If I could live in one room with a kitchen, that's all, I'd do it in a minute.

What will Madame V. [Valentina Schlee] do without her cook? She can't cook. I make my dinner every day. Sometimes I wish it would all come in on a tray, but I do it myself. If you can't, I'll tell you what you do: Go to a delicatessen and get yourself some brown beans—they're prepared—and some Swedish meatballs. Take it all home and have it with a slice of tomato—*fresh* tomato. It's delicious.

One thing I've discovered on television here are the cooks, especially one, I forget his name but he's adorable— I think he's adorable. He does these dishes—I mean he *does* them. If I could do just one dish like he does! Boy, he whips things up! He's marvelous. He scrambled eggs, and what he did to go with it—oh, it sounded so good. We could do that. Have you milk in your refrigerator ever? It's so easy and it

Garbo's eccentricities at table were the centerpiece of a *New Yorker* letter from Ravello, Italy, where she and Leopold Stokowski had retreated from paparazzi into the thousand-year-old Villa Cimbone. She had brought along her own pots of jam, which she "kept locked in her bedroom all day, brought down to the breakfast table at eight-thirty sharp, scooped ... onto her corn flakes, and poured her coffee over the mixture." Lunch consisted of two kinds of raw carrots, red and yellow, but "by three-thirty the companions were, of course, ravenously hungry again ... and Miss Garbo evidently thought that tea doesn't count as a meal. So from three-thirty till four-thirty, she innocently consumed enormous, fattening plates of cake and sandwich roll and bread and honey and jam." Stokowski evidently didn't—he claimed to be a purist who ate only tubers, and he chided Garbo when she had a case of canned string beans delivered to the villa.

After an early dinner of fruits and vegetables, Garbo retired for the evening, taking with her a bottle of olive oil and a box of salt. The salt, the servants finally surmised, was used for brushing her teeth, but the olive oil—well, they couldn't imagine, and it remains one of the smaller unsolved mysteries.

In 1955 Garbo returned from Sweden in a back-to-the-earth trance, telling friends that she intended to go off and raise potatoes and carrots. "The things which have to do with the soil are the only things which are pure, fine, and wonderful," she said. The following year she bought a thousand-acre estate sixty miles south of Stockholm, but as far as anyone knows, she spent little time there, never planted a garden of any kind, and eventually sold the property.

takes two minutes. Let's scramble some eggs.

I don't really know how to cook, but I never buy frozen food—I don't know what to do with it. I have some bouillon cubes, but I don't believe in them.

*The "outdoors type" rang true.*

Garbo never joined her colleagues in the MGM commissary, nor did she insist on catered lunches in her dressing room. She brown-bagged it, southern California skies allowing her to do so most days on the back lot, and the demand for news of her was such that details of her modest fare turned up in the columns: roast beef sandwiches, Swedish salami and Vasterbotten cheese, bran muffins with lots of butter, yogurt, codfish, potatoes. And lots of coffee.

*I* haven't had coffee in about ten days and I'm dying. Maybe I'll have a cup tomorrow and see what happens. But only in the morning can I drink it.

Can you make good coffee? I don't perk . . . I could no more stand and wait for a percolator or for something to drip —I'm not made that way. I throw the coffee in a boiling casserole and let it stand for a few minutes with a cover on it. Then I strain it and it's ready. Delicious . . . right smack in the pan. Couldn't be simpler. But we ought to have a nice, lovely Hindu man who comes and serves us, someone

147

Concocting tidbits about Garbo's domestic life, including her kitchen likes, a Metro press release failed somehow to make her sound as normal as blueberry pie:

*Likes corned beef and cabbage—and caviar!*
*In the summertime she insists on having ice cream cones served on the set warm afternoons at four. Her favorite salad is one consisting of vegetables and anchovies.*
*Prefers showers to baths because she likes to feel the water beating against her body.*

Gustav Norin, a house servant of Garbo's, was thoroughly quoted by Rilla Page Palmborg in *The Private Life of Greta Garbo,* published in 1931. Among his revelations: that he occasionally served his employer a "man's breakfast" in bed—chipped beef, eggs, coffee cake, coffee, juice —but on a pink enamel tray she'd ordered from a hardware store. "There were no doilies or dainty napkins," said Norin. "The plainer the better for her." Providing an inventory of Garbo's pantry and refrigerator, he recited her favorite menus and confirmed the fact that she had not lost her taste for such smorgasbord staples such as *bruna*

*bonor*—brown beans, baked with salt pork and brown sugar—and brine-cured lutefish, hardtack, and apple cake. "One of her favorite desserts," he revealed, "was sponge cake that had been dipped in wine and then covered with a thin custard. On top of that was piled some whipped cream, sweetened and flavored with vanilla and sprinkled with chopped almonds that had soaked in absinthe."

Often suffering insomnia, Garbo would wander into the kitchen after midnight to tear off a piece of the sponge cake, and drink a cold beer with it. Norin appreciated the fact that she was so tidy: "If she had eaten anything sticky she would fill the dish with water."

Palmborg was fascinated by Garbo's do-it-yourself practicality and lack of pretense, as if she expected the star would be lounging around with the proverbial box of bonbons. "It is a queer picture," Palmborg wrote, ". . . the mysterious Garbo stirring potatoes and frying a steak and then sitting down at the kitchen table to eat her solitary dinner, when all over the world there were thousands of admirers longing to set the handiwork of the greatest chefs before her."

*HER*
*SELF*

who comes on absolutely soundless feet and puts it there. Preferably, I wish he would come from the sky.

W asn't that fantastic? I wonder how many blocks we made —a hundred and twenty? I'm shot, absolutely shot. You know it was an enormous walk. I don't know how we did it. I haven't done that since the world began. The best thing is not to think, just trot, don't ask questions.

Y ou've got to keep moving—all I've got left is my bloody old walk. I couldn't survive here if I didn't walk. I couldn't be twenty-four hours in this apartment. The outdoors—sun and air and trees and the birdies. I love all things in nature, except wind. I can't stand wind of any kind.

A puzzling physical specimen, Garbo could seem both frail and robust. She struck the aesthete Stephen Tennant as "almost rude with insolent health," but she could also sigh and swoon as convincingly as any southern belle (Tennessee Williams wanted her to play Blanche DuBois). She often was ridiculously early to bed. Telephoto camera lenses caught her, in her sixties, on the terrace of her small apartment in the Swiss village of Klosters, performing calisthenics and standing on her head. In her explorations of Manhattan, she could out-hike junior companions, and she also proved her stamina in swimming pools and on tennis courts.

I haven't played tennis in fifty years. Somebody once many years ago said, "Here's a racquet, and you do this with a racquet." But I never learned anything. I never could play tennis. I never learned. And I could never play if human beings were sitting around looking at me.

How can I run around? I have no backhand. I can't run at all, so how can I get a backhand? I'm not that skillful.

The ball would probably go over the fence and you'd have to go out and get it.

John Gilbert taught Garbo to play tennis on his Tower Road courts, and she became a regular at Dolores del Rio and Cedric Gibbons's Saturday tennis parties. (King Vidor wouldn't say who won their match there, but he described Garbo as "a bulwark of strength" on the court, "covering [it] in long leaping gallops and strides, displaying a typical Swedish stubbornness and determination to let no shots get by her.") Garbo kept up her game after she and Gilbert parted, playing on Dolores del Rio and Cedric Gibbons's sunken courts. She celebrated the first screening of *Anna Karenina* with a game at Irene and David Selznick's two-and-a-half-acre estate in Beverly Hills.

"Garbo is all movement," wrote Louise Brooks of the star's acting technique. "First she gets the emotion and out of the emotion comes the movement, and out of the movement comes the dialogue." According to Sam Marx, each new role for Garbo began with the character's walk. "One afternoon I heard footsteps outside my office window," says Marx, "a pacing back and forth, back and forth. It varied each time, in the speed and rhythm of the steps. Finally I got up to look and there was Garbo in the alleyway, deep in concentration. She would do a length, stop, put her hand on her chin and puzzle there for a while, then go at it again. I realized that she was working, figuring out how her character would move. She was making *Grand Hotel* at the time, and when you watch that movie today, notice her entrance, the way she sort of floats into the scene. That's what I saw her perfecting that day."

Something's a little amiss with Miss G. at the moment. No, I'm not feeling very chipper, but I'm not going to give in. But I'm not going *out,* either. Someone wants me to come over and see her—she's feeling down and out. But I couldn't even answer. I thought, "Oh dear God, here's another punishment."

Are you staying in tonight or are you jumping? I think of other people and think, "My God, they know how to organize life's energy." The people I know, they're all functioning—if you gave a ball tomorrow night, they'd all be there. They go from morning to night, and I suppose they have a good time.

I'm not a normal man, so I can't do what other people do. If I could, I would be tossing around like the rest of the world and have something out of life. If you were made right you could travel, go for lunch, supper, go to the theater. But I'm not, I'm not made that way . . . I feel that I'll never move again, unless somebody lifts me up on a carpet and puts me somewhere . . . I get so tired. I'm as tired as I've ever been.

Profound exhaustion, spiritual and physical, was essential to Garbo's heavy-lidded persona. Indeed, an almost fatal fatigue was as venerable a theme in her art and life as the desire to be let alone. In her first scene in *Grand Hotel,* as the weary prima ballerina, Grusinskaya, she wakes from a nap and says, looking heavenward, "I think . . . I've never been so tired in my life." As Anna Christie, she calls herself "tired to death." Garbo was mag-

Garbo's own "health rules" appeared in a feature item of November 23, 1929, though the story—condescendingly addressed to the little people out there and clearly not in Garbo's words—was manufactured:

*Work with all the punch that you have in you. Don't shirk or watch the clock when you are on a job—whether it be typewriting, clerking, selling bonds, clothes or other merchandise, writing, acting, singing, or cooking a meal. Put all that you have into your work, and the returns will be one hundred fold. . . .*

*Everyone must work out his own system of relaxation. For myself, I have found the most effective method is to recline on a couch. I close my eyes and endeavor to relax every muscle. Then I try to think of the pleasantest thing I can and drift off, as it were, to "never-never-land." In this fashion tired nerves loosen, my body feels free and at the end of twenty minutes I feel refreshed and able to carry on again.*

An enervated Garbo
with director Edmund
Goulding on the set of
Grand Hotel.

nificently, sensuously tired, and was drawn to the quality in other people. Dorothy Sebastian played opposite her in two films, *A Woman of Affairs* and *The Single Standard,* and, hoping to establish a rapport with the star, told her straightaway how very tired she felt. It worked. "I'm glad you're tired," said Garbo. "I like tired people."

Even while living with John Gilbert on Tower Road, Garbo had no interest in keeping pace with her lover, who had the all-night energy of a fraternity boy. In Hollywood, she was the first to leave a party; and in New York, she always preferred matinees to evening curtains. But if not a participant, she was at least an occasional voyeur of nightlife in its many varieties; and if she

could remain incognito—and not be out too late—she might summon the energy to venture out to a few favorite spots: the Apex, a black jazz club in Los Angeles; the Peppermint Lounge in Twist-era New York; and, in Paris, a netherworld dance bar in the Montmartre.

*A*m I going to be in town Sunday? I'm going to be in *bed*. I'll be in bed with an electric pad. I'm going on the hot pad, but just one—one is enough, you couldn't possibly face two. I curl up in bed, you see, that's why I have a bad back. You don't know anything about lumbago, do you? If you haven't had it, I can't speak to you about it. Nobody knows why these awful things come and go, they just do. I've had lots of troubles with the back. You don't have a bad back? You're too young. I used to sleep curled up, that's the problem. I sleep better without pillows. It's a matter of getting used to it, and it's difficult if you're not. I never did sleep with pillows.

Now tell me—do I look very ill today? I look ill, I think. I *do* look ill—I look at myself and I get scared. My cold is always hanging—these poor little tonsils are just sitting there, waiting to act up again. The minute I get ill, I get terrified. I don't want to get examined before the holidays, because if there's anything wrong, then that's all I'll think about.

If Garbo wasn't a hypochondriac, she at least cultivated a hugely exaggerated sense of her own delicacy, and in a half-century of not working she had too much time to dwell on her aches and pains. A relentless seeker of sunshine and fresh air, she had a terrific fear of tuberculosis, which killed her father and her sister. As the consumptive Marguerite Gautier in *Camille*, Garbo is so ravishing that it is hard to believe she's ill until the final scene, when she suffers exquisitely—across her brow, in faltering movements of her body, and in the pained hush of her

Opposite: *With Robert Taylor and Jessie Ralph in* Camille. *"Usually Camilles do a great deal of coughing," said director George Cukor. "She just gave a very dry cough . . . [but] you knew that there was something seriously wrong with her. . . . You knew that she was dying of tuberculosis."*

last words to Armand: "It's my heart, it's not used to being happy. ... Perhaps it's better if I live in your heart where the world can't see me...."

*I* haven't got a thing to tell you today except that I'm not feeling too well.

You know, I have to watch it *all*—everything can hurt me. I read such an awful article about chickens, and of course that can apply to everything—pigs and cows, too. They say that our cows are eating all the poisons and other things out there. If you read what they write, sometimes, you wouldn't be able to eat, you'd just fold up.

For days and days once I ate only starch, because a doctor told me to. Only potatoes and spaghetti. No vegetables. Finally I said, "Couldn't I eat a banana or something that's alive?"

Then another doctor said, "Your worst enemy is starch."

I wish I had Bieler here. If I had Bieler, he'd give me yeast and water for two days, no food, no mercy. But Bieler's not a bore, not to the people who follow him. He doesn't have all the answers—no one does—but he's good.

In 1965, for the first and only time since leaving the movies, Garbo put her name before the public, by endorsing Henry Bieler's *Food Is Your Best Medicine*. The renegade California physician had an enormous following among, as his book jacket boasted, "star athletes, celebrities, and Pasadena dowagers." Garbo's testimonial, appearing alongside M.F.K. Fisher's and Hedda Hopper's, was not at all blurblike: "Having known Dr. Bieler for some years, I am sure his book will be a great help for many people in their fight against disease."

Though speaking out for Bieler violated all of Garbo's tenets of privacy, her friend Jean Howard, the Hollywood photographer (who was married to the agent Charles Feldman, who represented Garbo for a time), believes that she did so out of empathy for people in poor health. "We never discussed it, of course," says Howard, "but I'm sure the feelings came from the past, when she cared for her dying father. She knew how terrible it was to be unwell."

The book became a bestseller. "Glands fire the body," declared Bieler, whose recipes for long life included a well-fed endocrine system. *Glands:* a funny, indelicate word, one Garbo often used when talking about her health.

Since I was a very young man I believed that we are made in a certain way. Either you're born with very good glands or you're not. If you are, then you function very well. You can go out to nightclubs and drink, drink all night, go do whatever you want to do and nothing affects you. You're born a certain way—that's the way I've seen it functioning with me. Other people are wrecks. Come hell or high whatever it is, if it's not there, it's not there.

One afternoon on the set of *Conquest*, a baffled sound technician told director Clarence Brown that he was picking up strange interference, a noise he couldn't identify. It turned out that Garbo was to blame—she was in her dressing room, pureeing vegetables in a blender. "Garbo *lived* on Bieler's Broth," says Eleanor Phillips Colt. "We all did, still do. It's such a lovely, simple soup, a puree of zucchini, an onion, some other kind of squash, and potatoes."

Before Bieler there was Gayelord Hauser and his "hormone age" philosophy, linking diet and metabolism, exercise and mental well-being. Hauser, a survivor of childhood tuberculosis, dwelled on the glands, too, attracting followers with such teasers as "Indifferent lovers usually have a lazy thyroid." The first nutritionist to have his own television and radio programs, he marketed herbal preparations and advocated such "wonder foods" as yogurt, black-strap molasses, and brewer's yeast—and he was maligned by the medical community for doing so. Though much of his message was ahead of its time, Hauser could also come across as frivolous. "President Perón says his people need to hear me," he announced upon departing for Argentina on the first leg of an international lecture tour. "They're eating too much beef again . . . They need carrots." With books such as *Eat and Grow Beautiful*, and *Mirror, Mirror on the Wall*, Hauser cultivated an adoring clientele among the never-too-rich-or-too-thin set (he even named a salad for the decorator Lady Mendl). He won over Garbo late in 1939.

"I served these patties, and broiled grapefruit, to Greta Garbo the first time she ate at my house," he recalled in *Look Younger, Live Longer*:

"Two cups cooked wild rice, mixed with half cup chopped hazel nuts or walnuts, one slightly beaten egg. Fry in butter or peanut oil."

Hauser found Garbo's hair-shirt regime to be lacking in protein and also too restrictive and dull for an adventurous eater such as herself. He prescribed a diet that allowed meat, eggs, and cheese and Garbo liked the idea of indulgence in moderation. (Hauser's lunch menu for New York's Savoy-Plaza started with a gin-and-grapefruit-juice cocktail.) And she appreciated the fact that Hauser didn't harp too much on her smoking.

Someone once told me to buy a piece of ham, so I did. I never eat pork, or pork chops, ever, but this is prepared—in a slice—and very lean. It's absolutely delicious. Canadian bacon also is very lean, not fat, no mess. The other kind, the striped kind, makes a *cup* of fat. So if you get absolutely desperate one day, go and buy yourself a slice of ham.

I fry so seldom I don't even bother with nonstick pans. If I ever stoop to fry something, it's potatoes, and I fry them in peanut oil—*peanut oil,* it's a must. And you don't use a heck of a lot, just a little. No deep-fat anything, ever.

You can buy a little pan and a chop, a little steak, or a

little piece of liver and just throw it in the pan. It's not fun necessarily, but it's terribly easy. Terribly easy. Just remember, if there's fat on anything, cut it off. Even a steak to cook in my pan, I cut the fat off.

I cook vegetables in tap water, I drink bottled—they call it mountain water.

Garbo had begun work on *Ninotchka* when Hauser took over her life. Her easy manner on the set and her warmly funny performance in that comedy (her first since her Swedish debut in *Peter the Tramp*) caused people to wonder if the new friendship was romantic: "This Must Be Love Because I Feel So Well," ran the gossip-column headlines, mimicking the Rodgers and Hart song. In his "Tintypes" column, Sidney Skolsky broadly hinted that such rumors were way off, reporting that Garbo "likes Hauser but you can give odds, big odds, that she won't marry him." Louella Parsons, with unwitting double entendre, insisted that Garbo and Hauser were indeed "thataway."

In fact, Hauser shared a hilltop house above Coldwater Canyon with his companion Frey Brown, and they made a frequent foursome with Garbo and Mercedes de Acosta picnicking on secluded beaches. The *Hollywood Reporter* revealed that the two couples were sailing for Jamaica "to dine on pineapple, papaya and coconuts."

For six weeks one fall Garbo shared a cabin at Silver Lake with Mercedes de Acosta, who wrote of their intimate retreat, and of Garbo's athletic prowess:

*We clambered into the boat, and Greta took up the oars. I was amazed to see how well she rowed. Her stroke was quite superb. "Have you been training with the Oxford crew?" I asked. She rowed steadily and smoothly into the shadow of the mountain which lay reflected on the water.*

*With Greta's steady stroke we soon reached our island.*

*No one can really know Greta unless they have seen her as I saw her there in Silver Lake. She is a creature of the elements. A creature of wind and storms and rocks and trees and water. A spirit such as hers cooped up in a city is a tragic sight.*

A hundred-year lifespan was Hauser's goal, but he died at the age of eighty-nine in 1984. Garbo was in California at the time, and she attended the memorial service at All Saints Church in Beverly Hills. A gathering followed, hosted by Hauser's business partner Anthony Palermo. The photographer Ellen Graham was there. "Garbo asked that no one be there but Gayelord's closest friends," she says, "not even kitchen help. I knew Garbo as an incredibly sunny person. She just came alive when she visited California, and with Gayelord especially, but she was so grim that day, not herself at all. I thought she wouldn't make it."

Whatever I can do in the kitchen, you can do. It's all easy—boring sometimes, but it's so easy. Try it, I tell you . . . Any idiot in the world can do it. It's a small piece of business to fix yourself dinner.

But don't have a drink before or eat crackers and cheese before—it's much more fun that way, but it'll ruin the dinner.

I hear people say, "Oh, I never drink alone." Well, if I didn't drink alone I'd never get a drink. The people who never touch a drop would say, "You sinner, you're drinking yourself to death."

It's very necessary to drink, I've discovered. I love it. I have it every day, not one day without it. But only a certain amount. I've had this bottle of *glögg* for years and years—it's Swedish punch, very strong. It's delicious.

I just pour my bloody old whiskey straight. And you'll ruin a martini if you have too much vermouth.

Let's have a martini. I'm going to feel terribly guilty if you have tea.

Does Madame V. still smoke? How the hell did she do that? Ooh, but I don't think she inhales, and if you don't inhale you're not a smoker.

Actress Greta Garbo was granted permission today to bring in [to France] two hundred cartons of American cigarettes without paying duty after she told customs inspectors that she smokes fifty cigarettes daily.

—CHICAGO TRIBUNE PRESS SERVICE, JULY 21, 1957

I can't get off the cigarette kick. It's terrible. I've smoked since I'm seventeen and now my dopey body just waits for the next one. I smoke all day long. If you don't smoke, be glad—there's one feather in your cap. If you're an addict, nothing stops you. There was a horrible thing going on about smoking this morning on television, and you know I turned it off. I didn't want to listen to it. Isn't that awful—just like an ostrich.

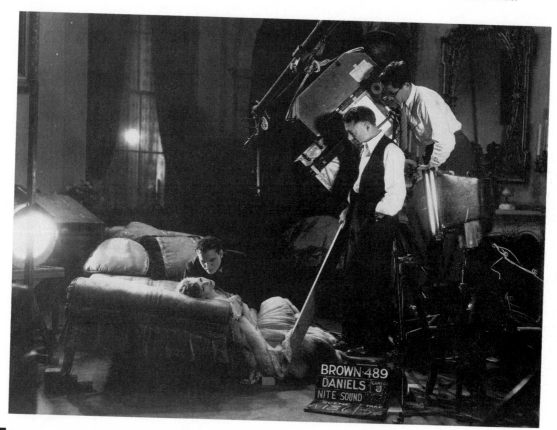

*In divine recline in* Romance. *Clarence Brown and William Daniels are behind the camera. To Bill Porter, who worked as Daniels's gaffer, Garbo was "peculiar but marvelous."*

BROWN·489
DANIELS
NITE SOUND

**I**f I'm sleeping, I'm sleeping. If not, then hell is loose. I'm a very sleepless man.

If I'm completely still and shut up, then I can sleep a little; but that's no way to live. Don't suggest that anything could help, kid. I'm still sleepless after five sets of tennis. Water lapping on a boat couldn't lull me to sleep.

I have at least forty sets of earplugs, but you can hear everything just as well. I'm an expert on earplugs. Mine are wax. I hear much better with them. I've worn them since I was twenty, and it does something psychological to you. You think they're going to calm things, but they really don't.

How do you get to that fourth state of sleep they write about, when you don't dream? Nobody can get to it without drugs. I tried sleeping pills when I was younger, but I didn't get into that again, because once you start, you're licked—it's on your mind that you can't sleep without them.

When you want to go to sleep, put your two fingers together, the thumb and the index finger of both hands. And then put your ankles together. Now you have a contact in your body like a circle. The people who are advanced say that you can control yourself better this way in sleep. Mind you, I give advice freely—I haven't tried it. You try it and I'll ask you about it.

7 THE WOMAN

Preceding page:
*Acting neighborly,*
*waving from one of*
*her rented California*
*houses.*

*I* don't drive, but I never hire drivers, either. That's not the way to be in California. When I was in the movies, sometimes I had to have a driver, but I tried not to. They sit there and wait and that's on your mind and drives you crazy, to have a man sitting there spending his life waiting in the street for you. I hate that. He'd rather be somewhere else.

People can be so rude to their drivers and to other servants. I know a couple of women who would say to them, "Go and get me that." I was shocked and thought, "Well, I never could talk that way." I don't think people who act like that will ever get out of it, because if you've gotten by all those years without knowing the difference . . . well, how can you, how can you change if you've gotten by all your life doing that sort of thing? It's another chemistry. It has nothing to do with California or New York. I've seen it in other countries. And it works—servants do more for those kinds of people than they would ever do for me.

Garbo may not have been generous in tipping, but she was consistently kind to people in service positions, perhaps remembering her own life as a department store clerk. In California she preferred to drive herself, but not if it made her chauffeurs feel useless, and she was always coming up with tasks simply to keep them occupied—deliver her to Santa Barbara, where she might buy tea, or drop her at Lake Arrowhead, seventy miles away, and return for her later in the day.

Garbo had been driving a secondhand Packard when, in 1933, she ordered a custom-built Duesenberg from Paris. Lew Ayres spotted her in the maroon convertible as she was driving along Sunset Boulevard one day. "The top was down, and I saw immediately who it was," says Ayres. "I pulled up right next to her and honked, but she didn't look up—just stared straight ahead. We drove on, side by side, and I honked a few more times, and waved, but she still never looked over. She never did see who it was honking at her, bothering her." A couple of years later Garbo was stopped as she sped across the Arizona desert with Rouben Mamoulian, but when the officer realized who it was, he waved her on, apologetically.

Garbo's Duesenberg sold at auction in 1987 for $1.4 million. The buyer, Jerry J. Moore, a Houston developer and owner of the Antique Car Museum, has put the car on display, along with a life-size mannequin of its former owner, dressed in a red velvet Adrian gown.

*T*here were marvelous places in California. I used to go to Lake Arrowhead. It was the only place I could go and be alone. I had a canoe and I got a little lunch box, and I used to land. But the last time I was there, you couldn't land anywhere—it was all taken by human beings. It was all sold. I tried the desert again, for old times' sake, and I must say it was rather boring.

For some unknown reason I've always wanted to see Las Vegas. It's probably horrible, all those people losing their shirts. Evidently they have a lot of places there, marvelous hotels, entertainment like mad. Imagine how crooked it all must be!—unless they take all that money away from the customers, how can they keep on all those shows and things? You have to get the money from somewhere. And with a lot of gamblers with good luck, they'd have to fix something—you just couldn't keep all that rolling. For some unknown reason I've always wanted to see it—I never saw it, in all those years I spent so close to it, in California.

People go like mad in California. There are always dinners and parties at people's houses. You go and it can be fun. At dinner you have to twist and turn as you speak. To mingle with the world, that can be lovely. But I don't seem to be like normal people—I start twirling in my head because I envy normal people.

*Garbo loved picnics, even on the job. With John Gilbert* (right) *and Edmund Goulding* (reclining), *on location for* Love.

Socially, Garbo either charmed people or left them cold, and the big question surrounding any event to which she had been invited was: Will she show up? At the prospect of meeting her, even the most accomplished individuals went a bit witless. But as

Tallulah Bankhead reported after her idol turned up unexpectedly at a dinner party: "If you don't treat her like something begotten by the Sphinx and Frigg, Norse goddess of the sky, she can be as much fun as the next gal."

Mae West also was smitten, though her account of their meeting dwelled less on Garbo than on West herself. According to West, George Cukor gave a party for the sole purpose of making the introduction:

> I said to a friend, "Let's see, what will I talk about? Oh, I'll talk about myself." And of course I did do most of the talking. I got there first and when Garbo came in I said, "Oh, hello dear," and kissed her on the cheek to make her feel at home. And then when she was loosened up she sat down on a very low chair. And I thought, "Oh, she's down low and there's a window open in back of her —she'll catch cold." So they closed the windows. And I said to her, "Do you like that low chair?" She said, "Oh, I'd like to sit on the floor." I told her, "No, you look good right there." I admire her because she always conducted herself well, didn't cheapen herself. She looked very good. I'd like to see her make more pictures."

Some less fortunate individuals encountered the pillish Garbo of a 1931 *New Yorker* profile:

> Six lively people were gathered in someone's Hollywood drawing room one rainy night when the doorbell rang and Miss Greta Garbo was announced. She came in wearing a beret over her straight blond hair, a tailored suit, a man's shirt and tie, and a pair of flat-heeled oxfords. When the guests saw her face with its delicate pallor ungarnished . . . their talk abruptly died away. She sat silent while they made sporadic comment on the weather and stole furtive looks at her. She was alone, bottled in by a childish lack of interest, inarticulate, uncomfortable, offering no access to herself. She was unwilling, perhaps unable, to share in the social responsibility of the occasion. She was indifferent to its human aspects. She had made the effort to come and now, awkwardly, she hid behind her beauty. The party soon scattered. Miss Garbo had frozen the evening.

165

*Garbo the imperious, caricatured by Nikolaus Wahl.*

*I*n California I learned about people—how to really see what people are. The things that are most striking are first of all their eyes and their tone, those two things: the sound of their voices—the way they speak—and their eyes. The way they move is also important. Those things make a human being. That's how you can judge if someone is a decent human being, and how gentle and relaxed they are, like the people I see in California. People are casual there, and go about their lives. It's all so easy.

After she left the movies and became a frequent visitor to California, Garbo was sometimes introduced by her friends as "Miss Garbo," but more often as "Miss G." or "G.G.," as if uttering the G-word would detonate an explosion. And she never simply walked into a room full of people. Ideally, she wanted to be in place—seated, drink in hand—before other guests arrived; oth-

Garbo never won an Oscar—her punishment, perhaps, for breaking so many of Hollywood's rules. She was nominated four times, twice in one year, 1930, for *Anna Christie* and *Romance* (the winner, for *The Divorcee*, was Norma Shearer—Mrs. Irving Thalberg). In one of the contest's historic upsets, Garbo's performance in *Camille* lost to Luise Rainer's in *The Good Earth*. Up again in 1939, for *Ninotchka*, Garbo was passed over, fairly, for Vivien Leigh as Scarlett O'Hara. In 1954 the Academy tried to make amends, as it sometimes does for its oversights, by presenting Garbo with a "special Oscar" for a "series of luminous performances." Asked by the show's producer, Jean Negulesco, to accept the award personally—if not at the ceremony in Los Angeles, then in New York—Garbo deliberated a day or two before declining. No visitor to her apartment ever reported having seen the statue on display.

erwise she would make as discreet an entrance as possible (to one observer, "like a crab—sideways"). Her dowdy "Harriet Brown" cloak (she even had matchbooks embossed with the alias) fooled only fools, though that is how she was presented to John Gielgud at a mutual friend's Mediterranean villa. After a few days in her company, Gielgud snapped, "Don't you think it's time we stopped this 'Miss Brown' nonsense? May I call you Harriet?"

Many remember Garbo as a cheery dinner guest, sometimes a flirtatious one ("coquettish," says her Beverly Hills friend Nancy de Herrera), modest but also totally aware of her appeal and her social currency. She could pitch in and be helpful, as when she played traffic director at a Sunday-afternoon party at Gayelord Hauser's, clearing congestion in the driveway; and she displayed a country-girl innocence in conversation. One of Douglas Fairbanks, Jr.'s favorite memories of Garbo is seeing her at a party in London in the 1960s, "at Claridge's—she was sitting there on the floor, looking up at someone, laughing helplessly at the worst jokes." A decade later, Garbo and Fairbanks found themselves near the same spot in the Mediterranean. One day at sunset Garbo, in bangs and sunglasses, smiled and waved for Fairbanks's camera; the snapshot hangs on his office wall in New York. Eleanor Phillips Colt recalls Garbo's "cornball sense of humor" and her liking for slightly off-color stories. One, lost on everyone but Garbo, had to do with a woman in Germany nursing her baby on a bus—when she sees that she's missed her stop, she runs off the bus, remembering to button her blouse but forgetting the baby. . . anyway, Garbo thought it was funny.

But you didn't have to laugh at her jokes. The only ground rule for other guests—and it was a tough one—was never to ask her anything about herself, especially about her years in Hollywood. In fact, it was best not to mention the movies at all.

The proscription of career talk was such that Gayelord Hauser at first considered not watching the Oscar telecast in March of 1982 because Garbo was staying with him at the time. But he finally decided he couldn't make the sacrifice. "He just *had* to watch," says Nancy de Herrera, a regular at Hauser's Oscar-night parties. "He said, 'I don't care if she *is* here, I'm not going to miss it.' " But Garbo joined in, too, and seemed to enjoy herself, commenting on the presenters, the winners, and the losers. Then—

*Garbo and Gilbert's
on-screen passion
was, fleetingly, the
real-life truth.*

frightful moment!—her image flashed on the screen in one of those collage tributes to "old Hollywood." According to de Herrera, the room fell silent: "No one breathed."

Bill Frye, who lived near Hauser, remembers Garbo being happiest working in the garden. "She was so tough, even in her seventies," he says. "She'd get out there every day to trim the oleanders and pull out weeds and yank out dead vines. Once she killed a rattlesnake with a hoe, and it quite thrilled her. When she told me about it over dinner, I was horrified and said I would've called the fire department. She said if it happened again to just call her instead. *She* would be the fire department."

When the rain is falling like mad I dress up and go out . . .
I always did that in California. I love the rain. Mad dogs and
Englishmen, and Miss G.

Certainly the somber Garbo and the energetic Gilbert were a case of opposites attracting. He actually admitted that he was in love with Garbo the star, not the woman. For a short while she no doubt fed on Gilbert's fabulous energy—and she was in awe of his earning power at Metro—but she must have grown tired of his insensitive displays of affection. (He christened his yacht *The Temptress*, after the movie that had destroyed Stiller at the studio and embarrassed Garbo.)

In Leonore Coffee's autobiography, *Storyline*, the Metro screenwriter describes overhearing a frantic telephone call from Garbo to Harry Edington on the day of Gilbert's marriage to Ina Claire. Similar accounts have Garbo crying to Edington, "Stop them . . . he's *mine*." Edington did not intervene, and afterwards Garbo made an icy statement to the press: "I hope Mr. Gilbert will be very happy."

During their fleeting romance, Garbo and John Gilbert were first-nighters about town, beaming for photographers and making entrances that drew stares even from the moguls and other stars—Garbo and Gilbert were that glamorous. She had moved into his walled compound at the crest of Tower Road, the panorama of Los Angeles below. Obviously Gilbert had not broken Garbo's restless, solitary spirit—her long late-night hikes in the rain, and her frequent vanishing acts proved that—but he did bring her out into the world a bit, as the screenwriter Frances Marion observed, "putting a brief end to her introspective brooding." (George Schlee would do the same for Garbo many years later in New York.)

At heart, Garbo remained apart, from Gilbert and all others, deeply solitary and inscrutable. "I like it when it rains," she told a reporter soon after she arrived in California. "Because when I walk in the rain I am separated from the world." Garbo echoed herself in her films, playing along with the studio's near-parody of her private life. In *A Woman of Affairs*, she spurns a flirt with a snappy, self-referential, "I am walking alone because I *want* to walk alone." Her eventual lover in the picture has a sailboat called the *All Alone*. As Anna Karenina she is told that she possesses "the divine gift of silence," and has the revelation that "one day, I will be—alone." In their screenplay for *Ninotchka*, Billy Wilder, Charles Brackett, and Walter Reisch trade on Garbo's severity, until she finally has a bellylaugh at Melvyn Douglas's expense. (Wilder says it is nonsense that the famous laugh was dubbed, as rumored. "Why would we need to do that?" he says. "She was a wonderful actress, after all.") Garbo and Douglas proved to be a sexy team in *As You Desire Me* and *Ninotchka*, and the studio paired them again in *Two-Faced Woman*. Early in the film, Douglas says to her (with a wink to the audience), "I want to be alone. Don't you know what that word means?"

For a short while Garbo lived in the 900 block of North Bedford Drive, across the street from Metro's Joe Cohn. "I'd see her coming and going—she took long walks every day," he says, "and we'd always wave and say we should have a drink together. I never pursued it. I respected her privacy. I knew she wasn't comfortable with many people other than Stiller, Seastrom, and other European friends like Emil Jannings."

Salka and Berthold Viertel and their friends—most of them fellow writers and artists, many of them Europeans—gave Garbo the sense of home she lost with Stiller's departure. The friendship developed a professional aspect when Salka Viertel joined Metro's story department—thanks to Garbo, who urged Irving Thalberg to hire her. For most of the 1930s, Viertel was charged with finding suitable material for her friend, a job she performed with varying degrees of success, judging by the Garbo oeuvre. She also served as go-between, conveying urgent messages to the star when no one at the studio, not even Mayer or Selznick, knew her latest telephone number or whereabouts.

Viertel recalled first meeting Garbo in 1932, at Ernst Lubitsch's house: "As was common in Hollywood, beautiful women were clustered in one corner of the room, while the men talked shop in the other. . . . Next to [another] star, whose billowing skirt was taking practically all the space, sat Greta Garbo. She was the only woman who wore an austere black suit and not an evening dress." Garbo liked the fact that the only film of hers Viertel had seen was *The Saga of Gösta Berling*, and the women enjoyed a long conversation, which continued when Garbo appeared at the

Douglas Fairbanks Jr.: "She lived near me at one point, and yes, I saw her take walks alone. But lots of people did that—it wasn't such a remarkable thing. I did it. Ronald Reagan did it."

Viertel house the next morning. "In the bright daylight she was even more beautiful," wrote Viertel. "She wore no makeup, not even powder, only the famous long eyelashes were thoroughly blackened with mascara. . . ."

In a series of talks he gave at UCLA in the spring of 1965, Christopher Isherwood, a friend of the Viertels, admitted to being as starstruck as any new boy in town when he first moved to

*Taking sun while filming* The Single Standard.

California: "We lived under the shadow of these sort of improbable people who seemed so remote from London. Like, for instance, Garbo. . . . I remember that we went to get a Christmas present for her . . . and when [Berthold] Viertel had to tell the clerk in the bookstore the name and address, [the clerk] just laughed, he couldn't believe it was being sent to her. She was such a legendary figure in those days, it seemed to be ridiculous that somebody would actually be sending something to her."

When he met Garbo, Isherwood couldn't help being seduced, according to his journal entry for April 7, 1940:

> I think [a mutual friend] is right when he says she's "a dumb cluck." She actually didn't know who Daladier was. If you watch her for a quarter of an hour, you see every one of her famous expressions. She repeats them, quite irreverently. There is the iron sternness of Ninotchka, the languorous open-lipped surrender of Camille, Mata Hari's wicked laugh, Christina's boyish toss of the head, Anna Christie's grimace of disgust. She is amazingly beautiful, so novel, so naturally compelling and commanding that her ridiculous artificiality, her downright silliness, can't spoil the effect.

Maybe young people who protest about bad things in the world are doing the smart thing, but they can't know about life—they haven't *had* it. But if they can stop the world from having wars again—I mean from *ever* having wars again. . . . But I don't think that's possible, because all people in all countries would have to refuse to go to war. Would we be restless if we didn't have wars, if all people had a nice, peaceful existence?

If you're not brutal, not getting into tantrums or throwing ugly words around or sticking out a knife at people, then there's hope for the world. Imagine if everyone had that decency—there would be no wars.

You'd think we'd do something to end war, to cut it off, so that your neighbor's son wouldn't be killed the next

morning. He could be saved if we would just stop. But nobody stops, and the son is killed, and the next neighbor's
son is killed—more each day. Those sons don't come back
to their families, and sometimes the families can't produce
more sons because it's too late. It's so sad.

What are we doing instead? Building weapons and making space travel. With all this going on in the world, so what
if we put up space stations or go to the moon again, tram-
pling on that earth there? They're fantastic, gigantic, unbelievable feats, but so what? If you could plant potatoes on
the moon or on a planet out there . . . But then you'd have
to ship them back for a few billion dollars. It's so silly. Well,
it all must have some meaning, otherwise it really would be
criminal.

I get so frightened by the news. There's so much disaster
going on—the oil spills mean the fish will die and the birds
can't fly. The air in every city has to get cleaned up, but all
they talk about are plans to do it. . . . It's something else to
actually do it. The machinery involved in getting measures
through is endless—the paperwork, the meetings, the
money. Meanwhile, we have to live in this environment. We
have to live in New York, and that's not terribly wonderful.

Garbo may have drawn a blank at Isherwood's mention of the
French premier Edouard Daladier, but it seems that she was
more politically astute, and involved, than any of her friends
could know. In the 1940s she was criticized for not going public
in the war effort, and it is true that she refused to make an appearance at the Hollywood Canteen—but who can imagine Garbo
passing out doughnuts to the boogie-woogie beat of the Andrew
Sisters? Salka Viertel came to her friend's defense when Garbo
did not join other stars in selling war bonds. "If anyone has made
the suggestion that Garbo isn't selling bonds because her sympa-
thies are on the wrong side, it's too preposterous even to be dis-

cussed," said Viertel. "There are some people who just cannot face crowds, no matter for what cause. Garbo is such a person. . . . Instead she buys many bonds herself [and] has done her utmost to help me in my work of rescuing anti-Fascist refugees from Europe." On December 12, 1939, Garbo wrote a $5,000 check on her account at the Farmers and Merchants National Bank, made out to the Finnish Relief Fund. According to various sources, including *The Man Called Intrepid*, published in 1976, Garbo was among the notables tapped for anti-Nazi undercover work by William Stephenson, a.k.a. "Intrepid," chief of British security in the United States. The several trips Garbo made to Sweden between 1938 and 1942 seem to have involved some secret service work for Stephenson, who had asked her to help identify Hitler's sympathizers in her neutral homeland and to prevail upon her influential friends—including members of Sweden's aristocracy and King Christian X of Denmark—to assist in the evacuation of Danish Jews. Garbo also may have conveyed information that assisted the escape of the nuclear physicist Niels Bohr from German-occupied Denmark. (Bohr joined Robert S. Oppenheimer's Manhattan Project in 1942.)

If these are the facts of the Intrepid case—and Stephenson never denied them—then they are among the more important secrets that Garbo took with her from this life. Some intriguing footnotes: After the war, Stephenson and Garbo moved into the same building in New York, living a floor apart at 450 East Fifty-second Street. And Garbo frequently made puzzling references to the late Dag Hammarskjöld, the Swedish diplomat and United Nations secretary-general, who would have had intimate knowledge of Allied intelligence operations in Scandinavia. Garbo met Hammarskjöld once, when he invited her to dinner.

*H*e looked rather strange. Do you really think Hammarskjöld was the giant that people have pictured him as? Physically, he was little; little hands. He smoked a cigar—maybe he wanted to look manly. He probably had nothing in the way of interest in the opposite sex.

He didn't make a deep impression on me, but you can't

judge by meeting a person once, especially since I was rather nervous. I hadn't read his book [Markings] properly, but at some point in his life, he said, he had dreams that he talked to God. That doesn't mean you're religious—anyone can dream that sort of dream.

There were some things that happened a long time ago that we had to talk about. We spoke Swedish to each other. It was very painful for me . . . but I can't tell you that story.

He died on my birthday. I remember that, because I only remember bad things, horrible things.*

"I had a fan in Mr. Hitler," Garbo told Sam Green, and it was true; it had been said during the war that the Führer's favorite movie was *Camille*. Garbo was appalled by the news, and announced that she would be willing to arrange a meeting with her admirer; if she failed to convince him to surrender, she would shoot him. The plan might have worked, as she told Green: "I could have done it. I'm the only person in the world who wouldn't have been searched."

About the increasingly theoretical idea of her comeback, Garbo was once heard to say, "It's up to God now." So many years without work and responsibilities, she grew increasingly restless and bereft of spirit. No one has ever described her as a religious woman, but Garbo, the worshiped idol, could not pass a church without looking inside, and she knew many along her New York routes: the Church of the Epiphany, St. Patrick's Cathedral, St. George's on Stuyvesant Square, Temple Emanu-El, the Friends Meeting House near Gramercy Park. She wanted to go in and be hit over the head by faith.

* Hammarskjöld was killed in a plane crash on September 18, 1961.

re you ever very sad? There's not much remedy for it. I wish to God I were in ecstasy about something. I'd like to get hold of somebody that's religious and ask them what they think of when they pray. What do they imagine? What's the image? You know as well as I do that there are people who are deeply religious and they are hauling in benefits from the feeling every day. That's no kidding. When things go wrong they are comforted. They just believe, and they're luckier. I'm going to find out what they're focusing on.

So many people believe without reasoning and they give it all to churches—it makes them feel good. But you don't have to go to church. If you have it in you, you don't need nuttin'. Imagine the money they could save building churches.

All you have to do is have it inside your small little chest. Otherwise it's a bloody old mishmash of brushing your teeth and going through the slush and coming home and having a whiskey.

I saw Billy Graham once on television and didn't give a

> In 1976 Garbo asked Jean Howard if she would accompany her to hear Billy Graham at Madison Square Garden. "I'm not quite sure why she wanted to go," says Howard. "She wouldn't say. But she got quite caught up in the sermon, and in watching all the thousands of people who came out for it. At one point she got nervous and raised her program to cover her face with it. But I reached over and gently forced her hand down and said, 'G.G., if you want someone to recognize you, then you just go right ahead and cover your face—that'll take care of that.' No one did recognize her, and she relaxed, and seemed to like what she heard."

damn, but then I heard him again and he was absolutely marvelous. I thought, "My God, he does speak well." He gets applause and I think that's peculiar—I don't associate that with a man of God. And it must cost thousands of dollars to rent Madison Square Garden. But he must have something. It's strange, you know—you can't convert someone in half an hour. But people sit in the audience and they come forward. He steamrolls you. He's a showman, that's for sure.

There is great wisdom in the Bible, as I remember. How many years and years and years ago was it written? But it sounds so asinine to take it literally, to say Goliath did this and Goliath did that. That was how many thousands of years ago? Are Catholics still explaining Mary and Jesus? I haven't read the Bible in years, but goodness is the greatest force in the world. Little details from the Lord keep you happy.

If I were assured then, I wouldn't be in such a mess, and fifty billion billion other people wouldn't either. If you believe life is eternal, you get on your knees all the time. But we're earthbound little creatures and we're not given to understanding what eternity is—that answer isn't given to human beings. It's too big for us. If you start at the beginning of everything, you're licked. We don't know why anything is in existence. We're not given to understanding tomorrow morning.

But if you have a belief, bully for you—you're better than the man who hasn't. I do envy people who have it—at least they have some anchor or hope. Bully bully bully. As long as you have a belief, then you're anchored, and nobody can take it away from you. What matters is the sureness that nothing can harm you because you believe in something and you belong somewhere. If you have that, then you're all right. Nothing can shake it.

What's important is that whenever you meet your fellow man, you're kind and you're decent. The main thing is if you *are* a decent human being—that's what counts, because if there aren't such people, then there's no hope for the world. Some people can murder and get a good night's sleep.

The only thing you have is the fundamental thing inside you, whether you take it into a monastery or onto a soapbox.

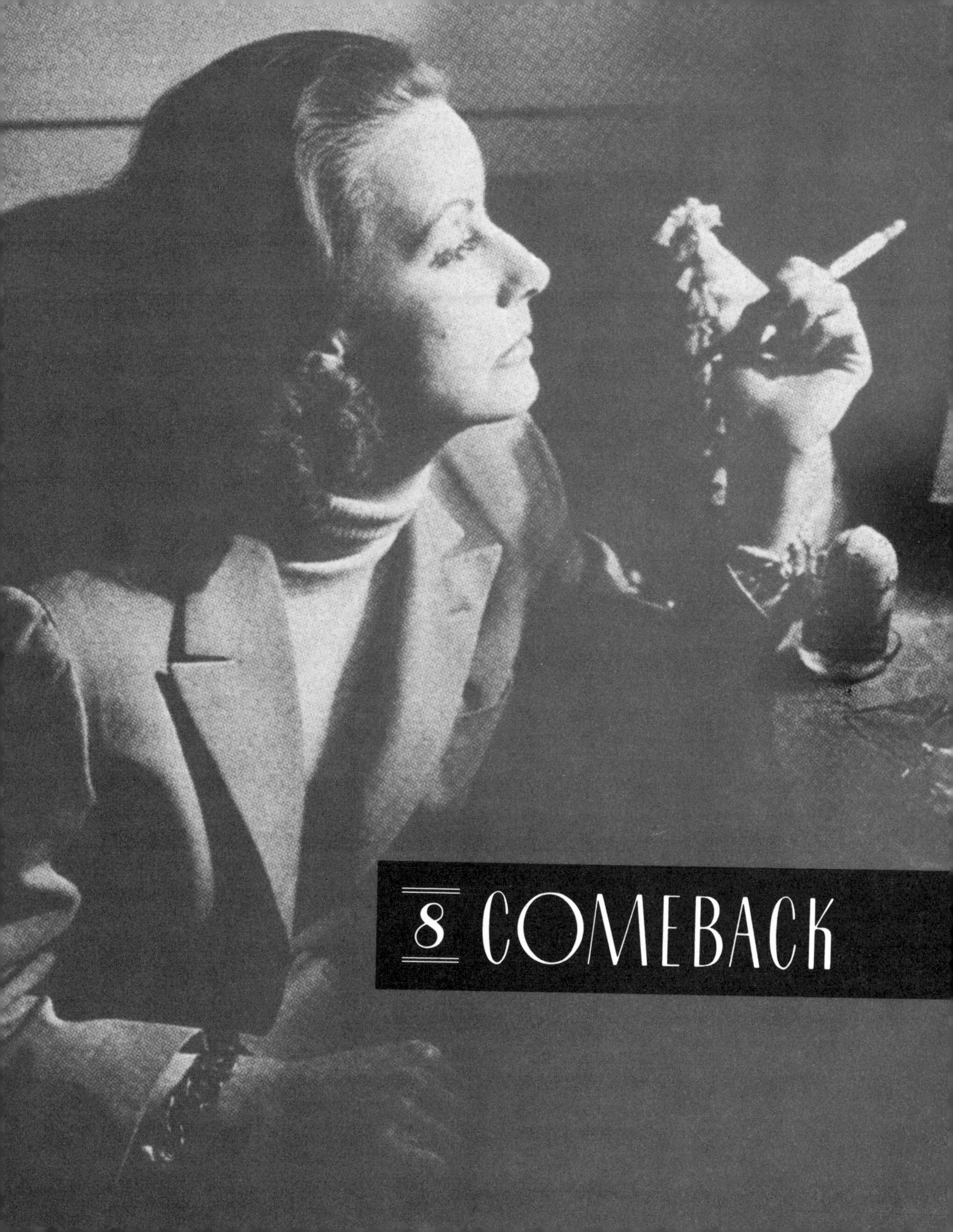

# 8 COMEBACK

D on't ever ask me about the movies, especially why I left them. . . . I mean, who would want a second term as President? I've dodged the past. Imagine if other actresses my age hibernated the way I do—they'd probably commit suicide. I'm sorry for a lot of things, for quitting things. But I've always lived my own peculiar way, willy-nilly. I'm sort of a free-going spirit, otherwise I can't exist. Actually, I've been out of order for years.

It takes forever for me to try to move anywhere, to make a move. How can I do anything when I can't even move from my living room to my other room? A friend told me, "You are like a mollusk." I didn't know what it meant, so I looked it up—it's an animal that doesn't move, just sits there.

Perhaps I'll give you a call, but don't sit back and wait. You know I never make any plans—I'll never get anywhere in life. If you can't make any plans, the other person gets upset, and so you make more plans, but they're just tentative.

In conversation Garbo's historic career was off-limits, as if the thunder had never happened at all. By insisting on that discretion from everyone, she came close to getting her wish for two lives—one for the movies, one for herself. There were moments when Garbo would break her own rule, recalling in a flash something or someone from long-ago Stockholm or Hollywood; but she remained detached from the memories.

Just as her avoidance of the media had made her that much more an object of pursuit, Garbo's departure from the movies added an enormous new dimension to her fame. How dare she step down from the pinnacle of success? To some it was shameful: Garbo was an ingrate who spurned the public who had adopted her and made her dream, the American dream, come true. To others her abdication was brave, selfless, and wise, leaving a beautiful illusion and legend intact (that is, she did not turn up in a *Berserk* or a *Bunny O'Hare*).

By the early 1940s, Garbo had grown afraid of the camera, of what it would see. Seeing her trotting along a street in Beverly Hills one afternoon, Billy Wilder stopped and invited her to come around to his house. She was taking her exercise, but that was no excuse to pass up a martini with Wilder, with whom she'd been friendly since their collaboration on *Ninotchka*. Once they'd put their feet up, he broached the subject: Would she ever go back to work? She said she would if she could play a clown. "She didn't want to show her face," says Wilder. "She wanted to hide behind greasepaint. The role appealed to her because she would play it in white makeup, so no one would be able to see her."

In the late 1950s, William S. Paley invited Garbo to lunch, having suggested through an intermediary that he would like to discuss a CBS radio production of *Anna Karenina*. She would be invisible, a voice. But nothing came of it; Paley never even mentioned the project to her. Apparently he had only wanted to be seen in Garbo's company.

> I think an artist who abandons his art is the saddest thing in the world, sadder than death.... There must have been something about [Garbo's] screen career that profoundly revolted her.
>
> —TENNESSEE WILLIAMS

Everyone had theories about Garbo's departure, all revolving around her vanity, her exhaustion, her boredom, her self-doubt.

But it was not such a surprising turn of events for someone who had abandoned Hollywood several times before, always hinting that it was over for her. "She is said to be going back to that farm of hers," wrote John Mosher in his *New Yorker* review of *As You Desire Me.* "Well, I shall wait and see, and occupy my mind, if possible, with other matters in the meanwhile, and try to endure the suspense." Garbo took little joy in her work and had always been ambivalent about her career, succeeding in spite of herself. "[I] ought to be grateful for a position that millions would thank God for," she wrote home at the age of twenty-one, dwelling on the miserable price of her success. As she had shown in her seven-month strike at MGM, she was not afraid to bow out, even if such action risked her reputation as a professional, and even if her behavior raised the question: If an artist stops working, is she truly an artist? Many have wondered what Garbo might have achieved had she dusted herself off from her last picture, *Two-Faced Woman,* and gone on to play the challenging roles that, in retirement, wistfully surrounded her name: Desdemona, Dorian Gray, Hamlet, even a clown.

It is true that *Two-Faced Woman,* in which Garbo sets a trap for her unfaithful husband by posing as her own twin, was an

*The unrecognizable "new Garbo" in her final film.*

embarrassing failure. She was anxious about the story, which was meant to jazz up her image. Watching "Garbo at her gayest," as the movie ads said, was "like seeing Sarah Bernhardt swatted by a bladder," according to one appalled critic. The film incited not only harsh criticism but actual condemnation, from the Catholic Legion of Decency. Led by New York's archbishop, Francis Spellman (the future cardinal), bishops around the country warned parishioners against the film, citing its "immoral and un-Christian attitude toward marriage, impudently suggestive scenes . . . and costumes." In an early scene that makes reference to a prewedding night spent in a motel, Melvyn Douglas says to her, "Let's go to bed," and they were shocking words for the time. Virtually every diocese in the country, and many city officials, debated the fate of the picture, which was banned in Providence, Boston, Hartford, Buffalo, and St. Louis. A Republican congressman, Martin J. Kennedy of New York, introduced a bill to halt the film's distribution nationally. The reaction was extreme, even at a time when the Hays Office and the Legion of Decency exerted terrific influence over the studios, and it may be that the censors had decided to make an example of this particular film: If the sacred Garbo could be shaken down, Hollywood might tighten up its standards.

Archbishop Spellman, in an unprecedented bit of secular interference, suggested to Louis B. Mayer that the film would be less sinful, and therefore acceptable for Catholics to see, if dialogue were added to show that Melvyn Douglas had known of his wife's charade all along. The new scene was shot and the film reedited, with the result that Garbo looks ridiculous, flailing around for a husband (and an audience) who's on to her trick. It was late 1941, and the war was on. After Pearl Harbor, the studio advertised the comedy as "a bright spot in a serious world," but even with the added boost of the censorship headlines, *Two-Faced Woman* fared poorly at the box office.

Though her worst fears about the picture had been realized, Garbo blamed no one but herself. She did not, however, as so many have insisted, renounce films at the age of thirty-six. Her exit was more gracious, and open-ended, than that: She simply released Metro from her contract. She soon, in fact, was eager to go back to work, according to a David Selznick memo of January

4, 1943. "I continue to get all kinds of messages from Garbo asking if I won't make a picture with her," he wrote to Dan O'Shea, an associate at Selznick International. "There is no particular reason why we should make a Garbo picture with all the women stars we have under contract—particularly Ingrid Bergman, but I will call it to your attention now only in case we run into a good piece of material. . . ."

Ingrid Bergman, who was beginning her remarkable ascent at Metro, had felt jilted when Garbo refused to meet her when she arrived at the studio. But in her memoirs, she wrote poignantly of her fellow Swede: "I suppose one of the saddest and most ironical things . . . was that I was just starting my career in Hollywood, and without knowing it [Garbo] was ending hers. . . . Can you imagine all those years, and you get up in the morning and what do you do? If you have children or grandchildren that's a different thing. But to be so lonely . . ."

In July of 1947, Garbo met Tennessee Williams, who very much wanted to see her back on the screen. "The meeting was arranged very carefully and privately like an audience with someone superior to the Pope," Williams wrote to Donald Windham. "She is still very beautiful. She drank straight vodka and said she would like to make another picture if the part was not male or female." Williams, in fact, had been working on a story, *The Pink Bedroom*, and George Cukor encouraged him to show it to Garbo. He did, in her apartment at the Ritz Tower in New York. "We sat in the parlor drinking schnapps," Williams wrote to Windham. "I got a big high and began to tell her [about] *The Pink Bedroom* . . . she kept whispering 'Wonderful!' leaning toward me with a look of entrancement in her eyes. I thought to myself, She will do it, she'll return to the screen! After an hour, when I had finished telling the scenario, she still said, 'Wonderful!' But then she sighed and leaned back on her sofa. 'Yes, it's wonderful, but not for me. Give it to Joan Crawford.' "

Some may doubt the particulars of this exchange, because the first part of *The Pink Bedroom* should have hit Garbo uncomfortably close to home. Williams never finished it, but his handwritten sketch outlines a weirdly familiar story—of Anna, a famous actress, and her mentor, a director named Stiller (Mauritz has become Michael). Anna is photographed by Arnold Genthe and grows weary of the press. Eventually breaking with Stiller, she hires a new manager, called Max, and their first picture is a great success, making Anna a star. The plot then departs real life. After the opening-night party, when Stiller finds Anna and Max in bed together, he kills himself—in Anna's pink bedroom. Ten years pass. Anna takes up with an effeminate incarnation of *Sweet Bird of Youth*'s Chance Wayne. Known as Dolores to his drag-queen friends, he is using Anna to launch his own legitimate career. Returning home one evening, she catches him prancing around in her ermine coat; after a catty exchange, he threatens to leave, but Anna—dangling a ruby-and-gold necklace before his envious eyes—manages to lure him into her pink bedroom. The curtain falls.

Skeptics who had no faith in Garbo's intention to work again were silenced in August of 1948, when she entered into an agreement with producer Walter Wanger. They were a good match, Garbo and the erudite Wanger, who had produced *Queen Christina*. Before they agreed upon a property, Garbo had said to him, "Please make sure that this is a good picture."

Immediately after announcing his coup, Wanger heard from George Cukor, who, along with other adventurous Hollywood filmmakers, was working in Europe. "I thought it extraordinary good news when I heard that you and Miss Brown had decided to make Cinema History together," he wrote, coyly referring to Garbo by her alias. "It will put an end to the terrible waste of [her] wonderful gifts and valuable time...." As excited as he was about the prospect of Garbo's return, Cukor also saw difficulty ahead, adding in his six-page letter to Wanger, "I shouldn't be surprised if obstacles were deliberately put in [our] way."

To find the right story and writer, Wanger dispatched his associate, Gene Frenke, and Garbo's friend, George Schlee, to Europe. There was talk of securing Jean-Paul Sartre to write a

Years after their sofa conference, Williams, who thought Garbo could play almost any role, turned to her at a small party in London, and blurted out, "You are the only great tragedienne that the screen ever had—you've got to resume your career!" It was an awful moment, as Williams conceded. "Garbo jumped up and exclaimed, 'This room is stifling!' She rushed across to a window, threw it all the way up as if about to leap out and stood there with her back to us for several minutes."

screenplay, or Albert Camus, or Somerset Maugham, or Colette. Defoe's *Moll Flanders* was discussed, and D'Annunzio's *The Flame*, Henry James's *The Princess Casamassima*, and the lives of Mary Magdalene and Eleanora Duse. Like David Selznick before him, Wanger was pulling out the literary stops for Garbo—who was not a woman of letters.

*I* never read *Alice in Wonderland*. Did I miss much?

*Gatsby* is short, but I couldn't finish it. I read thirty-five pages in two months' time. Dangerous things started to come up, and I couldn't read it. I had to put it down. Then I picked up Conrad—*The Secret Sharer*, of all things. Joseph Conrad. There's a man at sea, in his cabin, hidden. He's discovered a man, he's committed a murder, I think. They will execute him or something. I haven't gotten very far, but it makes me so nervous I can't read it.

I even tried *Airport*. It's a big book. It's in an airport, and it's a stormy night. Snow, snow, snow. It's petrifying.

That's it, you see. When I read, I get afraid that something terrible will happen. If nothing terrible happens, I don't remember it.

Somebody sent me a book, a publishing house. I'm on

the cover, but it's not about me, it's about a very well-known motion picture director who no longer exists [Ernst Lubitsch]. He was a marvelous little man, but I did only one little film with him. Why I should be on the cover I don't know. I opened the book two weeks ago and said, "Not today —mañana."

I don't want to settle down and read those long things. Lillian Hellman wrote her autobiography. Isn't that awful?

Garbo's library in New York consisted of multiple volumes of Thackeray, Hawthorne, Emerson, Fielding and Hardy, all bound in Morrocan leather and stamped in gold: books for show. Alan Elsner, proprietor of the First Avenue Bookshop, enjoyed having Garbo as a neighbor, but she was not much of a customer. "She'd

*Conferring with "that marvelous little man," Ernst Lubitsch, and Melvyn Douglas, on the set of* Ninotchka.

drop by every so often for a Swedish newspaper," says Elsner. "She'd plunk down her coins and say, 'That's to keep you in business.' I don't think she ever read anything."

But Garbo made friends of many writers—Huxley, Isherwood, and Maugham among them, and certainly she inspired a few. "Tell Madame Garbo that I had her in mind when I wrote about Elisabeth in *Les Enfants terribles,*" Jean Cocteau wrote to Roland Caillaud, who briefly was her neighbor in California. "[She is] Garbo at eighteen . . . I even put in an exact description of her features at the end, when Elisabeth takes up the revolver." Alice B. Toklas, however, was immune to Garbo's spell—she referred to her as "Mademoiselle Hamlet," and didn't mean it kindly. Garbo had offended her by taking a hurried glance at the paintings hanging in the Toklas-Stein apartment in Paris.

Walter Wanger was eager for Garbo to take on a great role, and he wasn't alone. After Louella Parsons and Sidney Skolsky reported the imminent reappearance of the star, aspiring screenwriters and fans deluged the producer's office with ideas and advice:

■ A Grayce Rodriguez wrote from El Paso: "Puleese—no modern stuff for Greta—somehow she doesn't go with bobby-soxer stuff. She belongs to the age of mystery, romance, thinking—when men and women knew how to make love and did. . . ."

■ From Martin Godfrey of Los Angeles: "A story for Greta Garbo? I might have one. IF Miss Garbo has the courage and the intelligence to play a woman of her age." To hear more, Wanger would have to respond; apparently he did not.

■ Arthur J. Dowling, a young Englishman, submitted his screen treatment of Virginia Woolf's *Mrs. Dalloway,* describing the title character as "much in love with the surface of life, with the parties at which she hopes (in Woolf's words) 'to create, kindle, illuminate. . . .' "

■ Joseph Zahorsky of West Aliquippa, Pennsylvania, trotted out a heavy repertoire: Shakespeare's Cleopatra, Portia, and Kate; Roxanne in *Cyrano de Bergerac;* and Hedda Gabler. But he added,

"Whatever you choose will be alright as long as you film it in Technicolor."

■ A Memphis fan was distressed to hear Robert Cummings mentioned as a possible co-star in the Wanger project. "Please inform Mr. Cummings that he is not fit to play opposite Miss Garbo," wrote John Hodges, who also weighed in on costume design and makeup. "It seems an insult to let Valentina do them. . . . [And] don't smear Miss Garbo with dry pancake and rouge. . . . Consult Paramount for la Dietrich's make-up formula. This Garbo film must *not* be second rate. If you can spend millions on Bergman, you can treat Greta properly, too. Remember, you have a trust, a duty to the world when you work with this nonpareil."

A year after announcing their partnership, Garbo and Wanger finally agreed on filming the life of George Sand. But before they could cast Chopin, they switched to another story, Balzac's *La Duchesse de Langeais*. Wanger was excited and intended the film —which cast Garbo as a decadent duchess who is undone by a love affair and dies young in a convent—to be a cornerstone of the Balzac centennial of 1950. Contracts were drawn up, and Garbo signed in her bold hand. She would have above-the-title billing, of course, and choice of director. Since the film would be made in Paris and Rome, provisions were made for first-class transportation and accommodations and "best available" meals. As it had been at Metro, it was written that her work day would end at five p.m. sharp, and she was not required to report to the set before nine o'clock each morning. Wanger's office assured her that "press relations shall be handled with fitting dignity." Though her fee had dropped, the remuneration was attractive: She would be paid $100,000—half of that sum during production, in eight weekly installments, and the balance upon completion. Once the film had grossed $2 million, Garbo would be paid an additional $50,000. If it made a profit, she would receive 15 percent of the producer's net.

George Schlee, unfortunately, did not restrict his duties to providing the reassurance Garbo would need to face a camera for the first time in nearly a decade. He tortured the business end of the deal, and pressed his creative ideas on the enterprise. Hoping that his friend Josh Logan would direct the film, he took Garbo to see Logan's Broadway production of *South Pacific*. Logan later recalled his dead-end discussion with Garbo and Schlee, whom he had agreed to meet in Vézelay, France:

"[Schlee] said, 'We'll meet you in the middle of the square—she doesn't want to meet in any big restaurant or anything like that, for fear some reporters would get hold of her.' And we went there, and I was looking for her. I thought I was going to see somebody in crinolines. But actually, the 'boy' that was standing next to me turned out to be Garbo. She looked just like Huck Finn, with a big straw hat, checkered shirt, and little shorts. We talked about *La Duchesse de Langeais*, and it was a hard story to solve, but could have been, with a wonderful screenwriter. . . ."

The German director Max Ophuls was given the job, but soon after cast and crew convened in Italy, Wanger reached his limit of Garbo's "embarrassing constant companion," as he referred to Schlee in a telegram to MCA. Schlee "formed a barrier for direct contact with Garbo," according to Wanger's wire, and was demanding on her behalf more money ($174,000, paid up front), a severely limited shooting schedule, and veto power over production design. Schlee also insisted on a six-month postponement, as Garbo was too tired to begin shooting. Schlee's demands, and Garbo's uncharacteristic display of temperament (so unlike her workmanlike manner at MGM), alarmed Wanger, who had no major studio backing him and threatened to "hold [both of them] responsible for all damages."

At the time Garbo and Schlee were running up a bill at the Grand Hotel in Rome, where she remained virtually unavailable to anyone associated with the production, even one of its potential European financiers, Angelo Rizzoli, of the publishing family. The paparazzi, who had jangled Garbo so badly when she visited Italy with Leopold Stokowski, were in a frenzy: "la Divina" was back, and behaving badly.

Addressing the Garbo tempest in her radio broadcast of January 22, 1950, Sheilah Graham said, "One of the conditions [of continuing the project] is that she leave her dressmaker [sic] boyfriend, George Schlee, behind in America. . . . Everyone said that Walter Wanger was living in a dream world and couldn't deliver Garbo—but [he] is trying hard to make Greta happy. He's trying to land Sir Laurence Olivier to play her lover." (If Wanger approached Olivier, neither man left any record of that. James Mason was cast in the role of Balzac's General Montriveau.)

All parties were back in the United States by February 17, 1950, when Wanger, in a stern letter from the St. Regis Hotel, made clear to Garbo his disappointment in her—but also indicated that he would be willing to work with her:

> When you said to me . . . you did not wish to make a mistake, and [asked] that I give you my word not to let you do anything I did not believe in, I took you at your word, alas! You even said it was not a matter of time nor money —you wanted to do a good picture or none at all. . . . I am only writing you this because I have always felt a bond of truthful understanding between yourself and myself, and I am not yet discouraged by the situation that others have forced upon us.

The collapse of the enterprise was humiliating for Garbo, for whom, for once, heaven and earth and endless dollars were not moved. Will she or won't she? Frequent rumblings of Garbo's reemergence were heard, especially after she became a U.S. citizen and settled in New York. Garbo herself kept the dream alive, tantalizing friends and colleagues. Twice she wrote to George Cukor, hinting of her desire to work with him again. In a typewritten, undated note, she assured Cukor that although she was mired for the forseeable future in everyday details of life, she hoped that he—as her once and possibly future director—was waiting for her return. (Evidently he was, for in her note Garbo also thanked him for a book she had not yet found the time to read; the title is not mentioned, but one wonders if Cukor had hoped to inspire her with a good story.) But in a handwritten note to Cukor, dated only with the year, 1956, Garbo indicated that she was unable to even discuss any film project with him.

Acting on Garbo's behalf, Salka Viertel and George Schlee approached David Selznick about a joint production with Svensk Filmindustri, of *Lady Chatterley's Lover*. Selznick was tempted, but finally decided to "toss up the sponge on it," fearing interference from censors. Garbo declined an offer from G. W. Pabst, who hoped to direct her for the first time since 1925's *Joyless Street*, in *The Odyssey* (Gregory Peck would star as Ulysses and Garbo

George Cukor was charmed by Garbo's "enormous distinction . . . and beautiful, beautiful manners," and they remained friends after she left Hollywood. "Garbo is a gentleman," he said. "She never says anything she doesn't mean. . . . When you're a friend of hers, she's very accessible and very sweet. Not always available."

would play three roles—Penelope, Circe, and Calypso). She discussed an adaptation of Daphne du Maurier's *My Cousin Rachel* with screenwriter Nunnally Johnson, who reported back to George Cukor of their telephone chat, "She couldn't have been more charming or adamant. She repeated her several emotional reasons for not wishing to come back into pictures and did this so winningly that I was presently enthusiastically on her side, in fact provided her with several additional reasons which up to that moment she hadn't thought of. The passion was so evident in my voice and manner that she quite prudently avoided any suggestion of a meeting in person. This was no time for any of us to lose our heads."

In 1959 Garbo obliged Anita Loos by attending a matinee of her adaptation of Colette's *Chéri*. Loos saw Garbo as a lovely, poignant Léa, but clearly the actress didn't like the play; all she spoke of after seeing it was her admiration for Colette.

On a visit to Stockholm in 1962 Garbo met Ingmar Bergman, who was tempted to ask her to take a small part in *The Silence*. In their brief meeting, however, the subject somehow never came up. Asked later why he thought she had left the movies, Bergman replied, "Because she was humiliated by Hollywood."

In a very different vein, Ross Hunter, in a lull between *Madame X* and *Thoroughly Modern Millie*, announced rather audaciously in 1966 that he wanted Garbo for *The Heaven Train*, a "religious western" in which she would star as a mother superior leading a wagon train of nuns across the country. "She read the screenplay and seemed to like it," says Hunter. "But she finally said we should do it with Katharine Hepburn." The film was never made.

In 1970, Katharine Hepburn, at age sixty-three, did star on Broadway in *Coco*, the Alan Jay Lerner musical based on the life of Coco Chanel. Garbo took in a matinee at the Mark Hellinger Theatre with her friend Cecile de Rothschild and was amazed when she heard that Gloria Swanson, at the age of sixty-seven, was hoping to follow Hepburn in the role.

*H*ow can they do it, these women? It's incredible. They're not chickens. How can they undertake such things? The mere thought slays me. I mean, it's terrifying—it's enough to kill an ox in a week.

Garbo loved Hepburn's performance, though she was too shy to visit her former MGM colleague's dressing room and tell her so.

*I* applauded like mad. I wish I could have gone backstage to see that one [Hepburn]. She can't sing—my God, she sounds like Rose Kennedy—but evidently she's full of energy, like Chanel.

Swanson lost the role of Coco to Danielle Darrieux (who in 1938 had been launched by Universal as a French Garbo), and later said of Garbo: "It's a pity that we aren't friends. I don't like a lot of people and I can understand her wishes to be left alone. Maybe the two of us could get together and she could come over and just relax while I paint and putter and do my sculpture— maybe she could do some painting, too, or whatever. We never knew each other in Hollywood, when we were both making pictures. Wouldn't it be a laugh if we two Swedes became good friends—what an item that would make!"

The most ridiculous rumor around Broadway one season had Garbo making her New York stage debut as a pantomime Pierrot —if the producers met her demand to clear the first fifteen rows of seats. The last whimper of a Garbo comeback was heard in 1971, when Luchino Visconti cautiously approached her about playing one scene, as the Queen of Naples, in his adaptation of Proust's *Remembrance of Things Past.* Said Visconti, who was unable to raise the money for the opulent production he was planning, "I am very pleased at the idea that this woman, with her severe and authoritarian presence, should figure in the decadent and rarefied climate of the world described by Proust."

As the idea of Garbo working again grew increasingly remote and fictional, a line from *Two-Faced Woman,* which turned out to be her professional farewell, resonated in a prophetic way: "In this harsh new world," she laments, "there is no place for me anymore."

# 9 ON HER OWN

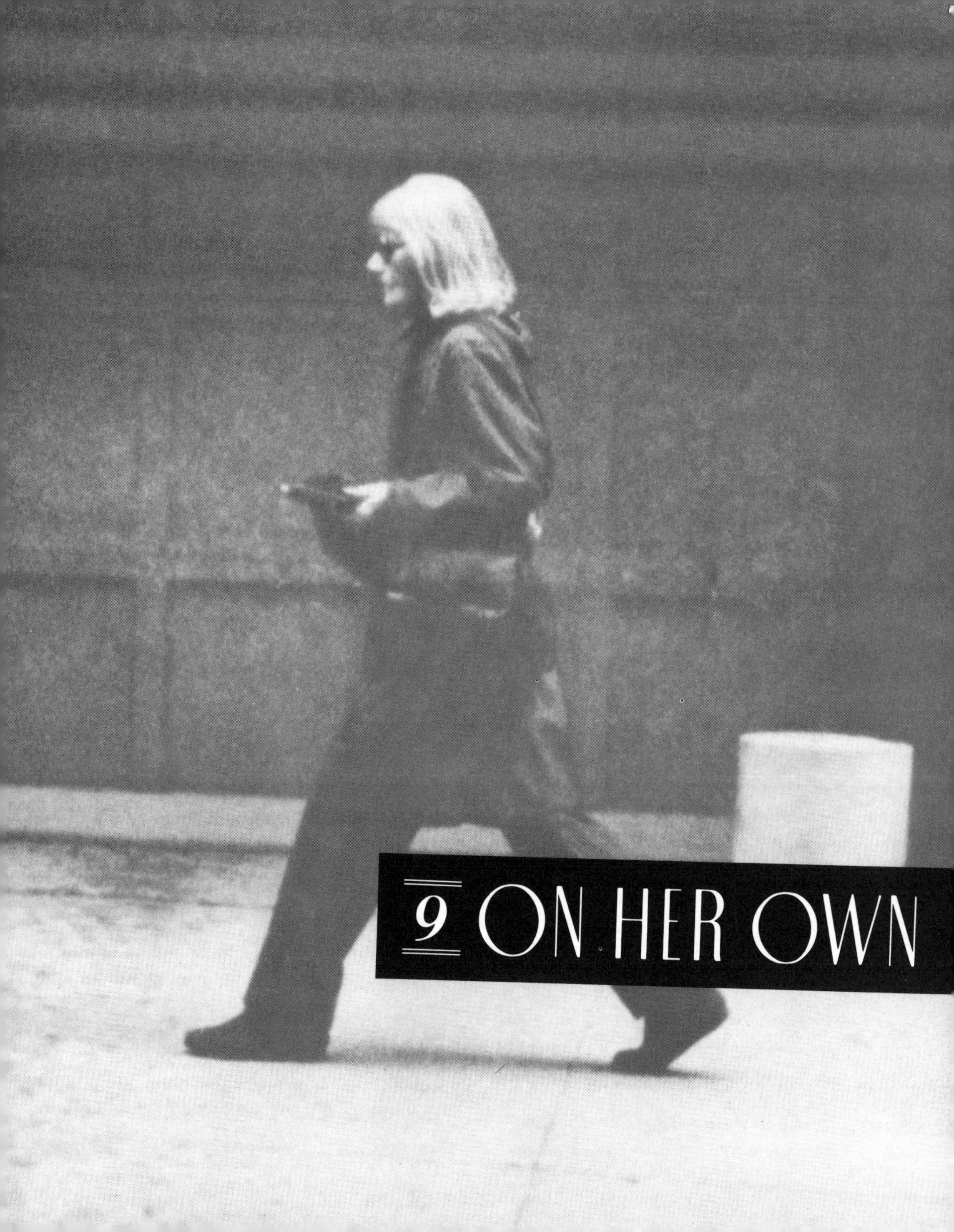

*Preceding page: For
four decades, Garbo
strode the streets of
New York.*

Somehow or other, New York is just not a very nice place now. It's convenient for me, because I'm in a building and there's a doorman before I have to go out into this horrible filthy street and go shop. Then I can go home and shut the door. But it's no life at all.

What are we doing racing through the soot and asphalt all the time? Isn't it fantastic, the way we live—human beings, born from nature to walk around where there's grass and trees and birdies? If you stop to think about it, you would go mad. Every breath of air is against what it was intended to be. Why we have to spend our whole lives on asphalt, I don't know.

And the noise is very dangerous. All of a sudden you jump five feet high, because something explodes or goes this way or that. It's all against your poor little mechanism.

I see in the newspaper, the *Post,* that "samplings taken during the last twenty-four hours at ten points across the city show that pollution levels remain excellent. Tomorrow continues excellent." What do they mean, "pollution levels remain excellent"? That's the funniest thing I ever saw. . . . Don't you think that's a mistake?

It's too filthy to stick your face out on my balcony to watch the boats go by. There's that giant *springbruhn* there, the Delacorte fountain shooting straight up from the river.

Isn't that silly, to want to be remembered by a giant spout of water? How do the boats get by?

I don't have to live in New York. I could live in hell.

Why would a recluse have chosen to make her home in the city of cities, among millions crowded onto an urban island? With her wealth and her disposition, why didn't Garbo do what Marlon Brando did and buy herself some real seclusion somewhere?

Certainly her early memories of New York were not entirely pleasant—and she'd often been harassed when she visited between films, on her way to and from Europe. Because she always was an inveterate walker, Garbo was easy prey to the city's reporters and photographers, who were of a far more aggressive breed than their Hollywood counterparts. They accosted her on the street, shouting questions: "Are you in love?" "Why have you left Hollywood?" "Are you married?" "Moving back to Sweden?" Registered as Gussie Berger at the St. Moritz during the Christmas season of 1931, Garbo was described as "a New England school marm made nervous by big-city surroundings," by one of the newsmen who mobbed her in the lobby of the hotel. She confessed her ill-concealed identity to the crowd, hoping the gesture would disperse them: "I [don't] want to be bothered. I came here from Hollywood for a rest, not to exhibit myself. I'm going back in a few days. I must start work on my new picture and until then I hope people will let me alone." As she boarded a train in Grand Central Station a year later, she sounded disgusted with the city, saying, "I don't see how people can live here and still breathe."

But in retirement, Garbo perhaps needed the distraction of the hubbub and the mass of human beings to mingle with anonymously in public places. Garbo was so enervated that she required the energy of others; in New York, she could live vicariously through the activity around her.

In California Garbo had been able to hide behind high hedges and within walled compounds, and her nomadic ways kept her a step ahead of the people who made maps to stars' homes. For some reason, there is no market for maps to their apartments in New York, where Garbo eventually got her wish not to be alone

but to be "let alone," as she once clarified it. Garbo sightings no longer made for hysteria—after all, she had not made a movie for a decade by the time she moved to the East Coast. But the name and the face (shadowed by her hats, half-hidden by her hands) still peppered newspaper columns: There she was, scowling as a crowd pressed around her car outside the Winter Garden Theatre, or looking pensive at the Parke-Bernet galleries. Her movements about town somehow were more than just fodder for gossip; for many, a close encounter with Garbo transcended normal experience. It was like a holy visitation. "I saw her today," a devotee might say, and "her" could mean only the great Garbo.

Approached, Garbo could be abrupt, as she was to a cheerful young man who bounded up to her one afternoon in the East Fifties, saying guilelessly, "Excuse me, Miss Garbo, but I'm a friend of Cecil Beaton, and I hope you don't mind if I introduce myself." Garbo walked briskly on, calling back, "I *do* mind." She seemed instead to appreciate silent acknowledgment of her presence on earth. Seeing that someone recognized her—in a crosswalk, at a greengrocer's, or browsing through a department store —she might nod slightly, give a small, conspiratorial smile, then draw a finger to her lips, as if to say "Shhh."

Opposite: *With Clark Gable in* Susan Lenox. *"Teaming with the great Garbo, of course, marks the peak of [his] vogue," said* Variety.

*T*he story of my life is about back entrances and side doors and secret elevators and other ways of getting in and out of places so that people won't bother you. But I do like Central Park. I always did. It's full of people with perambulators and things, so I find it pleasant.

In New York after the release of her only film with Clark Gable, *Susan Lenox: Her Fall and Rise,* Garbo sought refuge from autograph hunters one afternoon in the flower shop of her hotel, the St. Moritz. The proprietor, Arthur Tait, led her back to her room via service elevators and a maze of restricted corridors. "She was breathless, just a bundle of nerves," Tait reported the next day. "She threw off her hat and ran her graceful fingers through that beautiful head of hair and shook it in despair. I guess strangers terrify her. . . . But she was wonderful to me. She thanked me profusely for rescuing her from the public. When I got up to go back to the shop, she leaned over and patted me friendly-like on the back and said, 'God bless you.' Gee, you couldn't call anybody like that an iceberg, could you?"

Braving New York again the following year, Garbo attempted a quiet stroll through Central Park, which quickened to a dead-heat run from reporters and fans. Emerging on Central Park West, she hailed a taxicab, but before getting into the car she turned back and said to her pursuers, "I feel so sorry for you." To shake them, she took the cab to Bronxville, where she got out at an inn and called another car to take her back to the city. "Garbo Leads Chase Through Three Counties," chirped the headlines.

Later visits to the park were peaceful. Walking about one spring day with her friend Nadia Loftus, on the slopes just above the toy-boat pool, Garbo helped herself to a few tulips planted in a circle. Loftus, who was just as proper as her sister, the singer Jessica Dragonette, scolded her. "G.G., you cannot pick flowers here." Garbo looked up and said, "*I* can."

*I* had to go out on a little errand the other day. It was about a quarter past ten and I came onto Lexington and Fifty-ninth Street, where everything is. There's a little jewelry store there, and the street was full of people. Well, the store window was broken to bits, and the two poor jewelry men were outside without their coats, hats, or anything, just standing there, and an axe and a paper sack were lying on the street. Someone had hit the window with the axe, trying to grab something. So frightening.

I went up a couple of blocks to get my errand done and I came back. One of the men was outside, guarding the window, and I said, "I know people are asking you all kinds of questions, but did this just happen right now?" He said yes, it happened when they were inside—right in their faces it happened. Imagine, someone insane enough to take an axe and smash a window at quarter past ten in the morning on Lexington Avenue.

Can you imagine how strange life is? Somebody decides to hit you and get your money. They're sick, but then they strike people and make others sick, too. It's so ghastly that one can't even think of it. Look at the world, it's full of hurt. Well, I'm not a man with a desire to hurt another man. I can't do that.

You know if I see something violent on television I have to turn it off. But I was always disturbed by violence here. Imagine coming from Sweden a long time ago and to see first thing this woman running after this man with a rolling pin.

Garbo was referring to the warring Maggie and Jiggs of the "Bringing Up Father" comic strip, though she may have been no stranger to domestic violence herself. The truth was known only to Garbo and to her siblings and parents, but it has been suggested that her father, so often inebriated after his grueling night work, provoked her mother: The image is of a young Greta cowering in a corner of the two-room Gustafsson flat, pressing her hands over her ears as her parents fight. "If I see an accident or hear two people quarreling," she said in her 1928 *Photoplay* interview, "I am just sick all over. I never fight myself and I won't do any fighting in pictures." But in fact, crimes of passion, duels, and suicides over lost and unrequited love were staples of many of her pictures:

In *The Temptress,* Antonio Moreno is bullwhipped by his rival for her affections.

Facing off in the icy woods, John Gilbert, who has already killed Garbo's husband, wounds Lars Hanson in their duel at the end of *Flesh and the Devil.*

Sparing John Gilbert the pain of loving her, in *A Woman of Affairs,* Garbo kills herself by smashing her car into a tree.

To save Lew Ayres, her young suitor in *The Kiss,* she shoots and kills her husband.

Provoked by her abrupt departure in *As You Desire Me,* Erich von Stroheim fires a gun at Garbo, grazing her arm with a bullet.

Nils Asther flogs a servant in *Wild Orchids*, and though horrified by his cruelty, Garbo falls for him anyway.

She bashes in the head of a brutish Alan Hale in *Susan Lenox*.

As Mata Hari, she shoots Lionel Barrymore, and, true to life, faces a firing squad.

New York was the ideal in-between place for one who traveled so frequently to California and Europe. Like many New Yorkers, Garbo talked a lot about other, better places to live. Not even the dreaded necessity of showing her passport grounded her, though she did segregate herself from her fellow travelers as much as possible, often booking two first-class seats for herself and paying for all the VIP insulation that exists. She did not endear herself to other passengers on ocean liners, hiding away in her cabins, making much to do of her secret boardings and disembarkings, and asking for special favors—that sun decks and swimming pools be cleared for her exclusive use, for example. When she didn't get her way—and business practices usually ensured that she didn't—Garbo would take her nude sunbaths (and sometimes her meals) in lifeboats.

She had experienced the thrill of travel at an early age, as the head of Mauritz Stiller's entourage; and to a poor Swedish girl, California must have seemed as exotic as Constantinople. "My people do not realize how short the world is, that you can go by boats and trains," she said at the age of twenty-two. "I would like to just have enough money to travel. I have no place I want to go, except back to Sweden." Then, after a pause: "I want to go every place!"

New York is getting stranger and stranger, but I have no idea where one can go. Just running around all night trying to find somewhere to sleep, though that's not what I'm looking for. I don't know places. If only you knew how little I've seen of Europe. Nobody can believe it.

There are so many places in America, if one only knew where to go. It's horrible not to have a place to go to, but how does one get to finding a place? I couldn't go anywhere

Opposite: *Garbo, a bleached blond in* As You Desire Me, *admired Erich von Stroheim, considered by the studios to be the most difficult man in Hollywood. He played her nemesis in the film.*

that was elegant and you had to dress up and face people. I hate being a guest. I wouldn't go to Buckingham Palace if you gave me a million dollars.

I've been talking about going away for two months, but I won't do it. If I were very sociable I could ask my neighbors about leaving New York. Mary Martin lives here and she went somewhere and said it was very enjoyable—I read about it in an interview somewhere. But I'm not a normal man and I can't do what other people do.

It's easy for normal human beings—they just pick a car and go, and they land somewhere. Or you find your deck chair and sit there and look at an island. It would probably be pleasant, I'm sure of it. But I'm not made that way, you see. If somebody knows you, then you're a target, and if they want to approach you, you can't escape anywhere. I want the least that anybody sees you—that's my main thing.

I did go to New Jersey. The air is so much better and the snow on the ground there is clean, so clean. I don't know anything about New Jersey but that one little place I've been to. It's little houses next to one another, but God, it's clean snow!

They don't have taxes there, or they pay only on property or something, not like we have here. All the criminals live there apparently.

*I*'m a rather unreliable human being. As a traveling companion I don't recommend myself—I'm too much of a menace. I'm not much company because when the evening descends I usually disappear. I wouldn't have breakfast with you, either. Lunch and the whole day, but no morning and no evening. If you think you're going to have company all day I may as well tell you now, you're not. You'd be saying,

Asked in Hollywood about her schooling, Garbo replied, honestly, that she'd done well in all subjects except for geography, saying, "I was afraid of the map."

"Hell, what do I do all day by myself?" So I don't recommend myself. It's not too good to go with maniacs.

> Over the years Garbo recruited several traveling companions —Gayelord Hauser, George Schlee, Cecile de Rothschild, Mercedes de Acosta, Cecil Beaton, her niece Gray Reisfield—but she always liked the idea of traveling alone. As she asserted in her teens, "I would not care for company. . . . It is not necessary to have company when you travel."

Y̲ou call the airlines yourself? How do you do that? I'd be so scared, I'd be so nervous.

I have a map, but I can't read it—I don't know why the hell I look. I don't have any knowledge there—my geography is *nichts*. I can't even leave a building without turning left when I should turn right. And I can't remember about time changes, that's the kind of man I am.

> "I want to go . . . into the hills of China, to Japan. The Chinese and the Japanese have such strange faces. I wonder what must be inside of them. I would like to touch in China the little things that have been so many thousands of years on earth."
>
> —GARBO, MAY 1928

Y̲ou tell me that Hawaii had no sun—oh dear, another illusion gone. Have you investigated more about Jamaica? Or was it Grenada? Oh, what's in a name—that's the only thing I remember about Shakespeare.

And what did this human being say Grenada was at all good for? The Spice Island Hotel . . . eighty-six degrees at Christmas . . . ooh la la, that's as good as hell. But beaches are not for me, not in places like Jamaica. Places like that are just booked up. Maybe Puerto Rico has a nice stretch of beach and maybe no one goes there.

I've been to Barbados, and it takes a heck of a long time to get there. There's not very good swimming in Barbados, unless you go to a few tiny spots. I don't play tennis fantastically well, or swim very well, just enough to get by, and I don't ride a bicycle—that I could never learn. I skated as a child and got bowlegged and fell off and never tried it again. Skating, bicycling—that is *out*.

> "That weekend visit of Greta Garbo to the Pines at Fire Island—it had everyone there more a-twitter than usual.... Gee-Gee was in hiding most of the weekend but she did come out of seclusion one evening to dine at the Sandpiper and to shop at the Three B's Boutique. And she popped into the community grocery store. Doesn't it sound heaven?"
>
> —"SUZY SAYS," JULY 28, 1968

You take the easiest way out of New York and you go.

I'm thinking of going back to where I used to go, to this little village in Switzerland. I haven't seen the sun there in two years, and it's so boring—it would kill any human being except me. I've gone to Klosters for years, and if you'd come and see where I dwell, you wouldn't believe it. I spend three months in Switzerland, living exactly as I do here, making my own meals, staying in a little apartment. I go walking, that's all. There's hardly anybody who could take that, but I'm so abnormal I shouldn't even mention my name on the same day as other people. I don't really see people there, just one friend, every day, and the rest I'm alone.

It's dreary, but at least it's a place to get out of the New York soot in the summer. It gets you off Fifth Ave. What is life anyway? It's small details—that's all it amounts to. You think you missed something, because it's not really exciting.

Luckily I have help with my place. Living alone on one floor, I couldn't do it all myself. I'd just be cleaning all the time. If I didn't have anybody to help, then I'd be in one room with a kitchen. A bachelor's flat. I'd do it in a minute.

I'm lucky to be in my building. They don't like actresses there.

Making the commitment to settle in New York did not come easily to Garbo, a self-described wanderer since making her exit from MGM in 1941. "I have no plans," she said at the end of that decade, when she was living out of trunks and suitcases at the Ritz Tower. "I have no place . . . I'm sort of drifting." By 1950 she was renting rooms at Hampshire House, on Central Park South, and it was reported that her friend Eric de Rothschild-Goldschmidt was advising her on purchases of eighteenth-century French furniture. She had a special fondness for gilt-edged Louis XVI *fauteuils*, made in pairs, and richly uphol-stered *bergères*, and the acquisitions struck some as peculiar, since she had no real home for them. She still had not been able to answer the question of where she would like to live—the United States or Sweden. "I'm frightfully divided between the two," she told a reporter who scored a few-second interview at one of her many disembarkings at the Hudson River piers. (Garbo allowed that her trip had been a vacation. From *what*, was the rude question. No answer was given.) Her indecision ended on February 9, 1951, when she joined a hundred and fifty other ap-plicants at the Bureau of Immigration and Naturalization, taking the oath of allegiance and signing citizenship papers. Not lifting the dark veil over her hat, Garbo mustered a few words as she made her way back to the car of her unidentified escort: "I am glad to become a citizen of the United States."

*Ending years of indecision, Garbo signed her U.S. citizenship papers in 1951.*

Garbo moved for the last time in 1953, into the fifth-floor apartment of 450 East Fifty-second Street. The Campanile is a stone tower almost as slender as its namesake (though there are no bells at its summit). It is a strange architectural hybrid, built in 1927, owing something to a Norman chateau and even more to a Venetian palazzo, especially when viewed from its terraced boat landing on the East River. Henry Luce lived there in the 1930s, in what his detractors called "the Monster's Palace." Garbo's comment about the cooperative board not liking actresses in the building was made jokingly, for her fellow residents welcomed her into the building. Mary Martin had the penthouse, and Ethel Barrymore had lived in the three-story apartment that included Alexander Woollcott's bachelor quarters (later Noel Coward's), and it was the drama critic's rollicking tenure in the cul-de-sac of East Fifty-second that inspired Dorothy Parker's sobriquet for it: Wit's End. The dead-end block, with its view of the East River and FDR Drive, provided a measure of privacy for Garbo, but took away another: Except by boat, there is only one way out of the street, and to get a shot at her, photographers simply had to post themselves at a corner of First Avenue and wait for her to emerge.

There is virtually no public space in the apartment house, only a dimly lit, stone-floored vestibule furnished with two iron chairs, a marble-topped table, and a black-framed mirror. "All Visitors Must Be Announced" seems immensely understated here. For many years, Garbo's residency was indicated simply by a "G" on the intercom; eventually, the telltale letter was removed. Asked if she lived there, doormen would indicate that she did without actually saying so. Accepting letters or packages for her, they could not guarantee that they would be opened, only that they would be delivered to the fifth floor and left on the table outside her door.

Admittance into the Garbo sanctuary was so rare a privilege that it made trespassers and liars out of those not invited in. Josh Logan confessed that he had virtually pushed his way into the apartment after escorting Garbo home from a party one night. He recorded what he saw:

"We first stepped into a small, empty hall, shiningly clean as though someone had waxed it a few minutes before. There were two doors open off this hallway and as we passed them I glanced in and saw two empty rooms—again spotlessly clean—but truly empty, without a single picture, rug, or piece of furniture.

"On the other side of the hallway the door was closed. That must have been Garbo's own bedroom and bath."

But then Logan turned into an opulent, rose-colored drawing room. Scanning the walls, he recognized a Renoir among many paintings.

Another guest, at least a purported one, was Truman Capote, who wrote unkindly of Garbo in *La Côte Basque:* "I saw her last night at the Gunthers' and I must say the whole set-up has taken on a very weathered look, dry and drafty, like an abandoned temple, something lost in the jungles at Angkor Wat; but that's what happens when you spend most of a life loving only yourself, and that not very much." Why such a sting? Had Garbo once spurned Capote? He later described her apartment, quite accurately, as "five large rooms with high windows." They were, he wrote, a "disconnected jumble" of chairs, tables, couches, and curtains. "It looks as if several decorators had worked on the job simultaneously, each with a different point of view....The overall impression is astonishing, but pleasant in a somewhat gaga way."

But then Capote showed his hand, claiming there was no television set in the apartment. Obviously, Garbo had never extended an invitation to him.

She did watch television, in bed and unapologetically, and warbled her own renditions of game-show themes and commercial jingles.

*I*'m not onto highbrow things. I watch the dreck. *Schmutz*. If a program is advertised as experimental, or special, I never turn it on. If you only knew what trash I look at on television. Very dreary. I'm the same way with music. You say Mozart puts the world right for you. Nothing like that would put me right. I wouldn't give it a chance. Mozart's not for me.

I just listen to mediocre television. I'm caught in it. But my reception is bad. I look at Channel 13 and it's completely goofy. I can't see anything, just flickerings. Channel 2 comes in well—the lower ones come in better. See, if you cater to the lower things in life, you get somewhere.

I do want to watch *David Copperfield* on television tonight. Oh, it's a marvelous cast—Richardson, Olivier, and Redgrave. They're all males. Marvelous cast. I thought I'd put it on for a little while but they're showing it too late. Why can't they put it on at a decent hour for me? You know what I call late, six o'clock or so. I get too upset, I get off-key again if I watch television too late.

I always wanted to see *Becket* again, but they put it on television so late at night that I can't watch it, because I'm a limited man. I saw it once in a movie theater. I was in a trance—I thought it was absolutely beautiful, in a haunting way. It's obviously homosexual between the two men. I always wanted to see it again, but television will have to change before that can happen. Oh, what a funny man I am.

Valentina and George Schlee also lived in the Campanile, and it was no accident that Garbo wound up at the same address. Since meeting Garbo at his wife's couture studio in 1948, George Schlee had taken over her life. He was the Mauritz Stiller of her middle age, grooming her as international, untouchable legend and securing her wealth in sound investments. Schlee was eager to see Garbo settled in a proper place, and when the fifth floor of the Campanile became available, he expedited her purchase of it. Together, the Schlees helped Garbo decorate the apartment, emphasizing her favorite shades of rose.

What does Madame V. look at when she prays? She's forever praying and lighting candles and crossing herself. But how can she behave the way she does? If I had kept seeing her I wouldn't be alive today.

It was so curious that she was downstairs when we came in—I was so nervous that she'd be unpleasant with you later. One second with Valentina could be hell.

You say she was friendly the other evening? What happened? If she were that friendly all the time, it'd be marvelous. Couldn't tear yourself away.

There was more to this threesome than just friendship; but if they began as a ménage à trois, as many believe, Valentina was soon made to feel that she was crowding the other two. Though she at first appeared blasé, making herself scarce on the days Garbo wanted to spend with George in the Schlees' ninth-floor apartment, Valentina was getting hot under her turbans. (According to a fashion-magazine editor, the horror of the situation hit Valentina when Garbo joined her and George in Venice in 1957. Awakening one morning Valentina was completely bald: Her long red hair had fallen out overnight.)

Garbo never became the great hostess Schlee wanted her to be, but the "former actress," as news dispatches now tagged her, was at least alive and living well: as a guest on Aristotle Onassis's yacht; shopping on the Via Veneto in Rome, taking a fifth-row seat at the Haymarket Theatre in London, sharing bottles of vin ordinaire with friends in Capri, or swimming off "The Rock," the Schlee villa on the Côte d'Azur. Schlee even lured Garbo to Washington, for a dinner at the Kennedy White House. When they arrived at their hotel that evening, however, Garbo tried to back out; though she admired John F. Kennedy, she was simply too nervous to face him. Schlee, familiar with such last-minute panic and equivocation, gave her an ultimatum: If she must cancel, fine, but she would have to admit herself into a hospital so that he could make a credible excuse. Faced with that scenario, Garbo composed herself and dressed for dinner. The evening went beautifully, Garbo chatting easily with the President, and she was delighted when he showed her around and told her she could come back anytime for a swim in the White House pool. Garbo admitted to Sam Green that she may have enjoyed herself too much at the White House tour. At one point, she told him, she bounced up and down on the Lincoln Bed—a bit of playfulness, she feared, that Jacqueline Kennedy did not appreciate.

As she grew more dependent on Schlee, Garbo cut others short to make time for him, and she waited for his telephone calls. She once rushed off after a late lunch with Billy Baldwin, giving a baffling excuse having to do with Schlee. "You know I have to leave you now," she told Baldwin. "He knows where I am, and I'd rather not be seen with you or anybody here because he is a gentleman and it wouldn't be a good idea."

On October 4, 1964, in the suite he and Garbo were sharing at the Crillon Hotel in Paris, George Schlee suffered a fatal heart attack. He was sixty-three. Garbo did not behave nobly, fleeing to a Rothschild estate outside of Paris. Valentina, who arrived from New York for her husband's body, now dropped her mask. She would never again utter Garbo's name, referring to her instead as "the vampire" or simply as "the fifth floor."

Schlee's obituary in the *New York Times* identified him as a "longtime associate and business advisor to Greta Garbo," and reviewed his early life of privilege in St. Petersburg, before he and the seventeen-year-old Valentina fled the Red Army in 1920. To stay alive, as Schlee had often said of their saga, "we ate our diamonds." Valentina, in a black dress and veil of her own design, led the mourners, who included Noel Coward, Bennett Cerf, Anita

Loos, and Lillian Gish. John Gunther spoke at the funeral, saying, "It is hard to talk about George, for he leaves no public record. He was just a delightful human being, a connoisseur of the art of living, a warm and sincere man." Though she was back in New York, Garbo did not attend the service. After burying Schlee, Valentina ordered custodians at Ferncliff Cemetery in Westchester County to prohibit Garbo from entering the premises.

The most conspicuous jewelry Valentina had ever worn were her silver and gold crosses, and she now took her Russian Orthodoxy over the top, summoning a priest to exorcise Garbo's spirit from the apartment (including the inside of the refrigerator). She also instructed doormen and operators of the building's one elevator to do all they could to keep her from ever encountering "the monster." One evening, they failed: Valentina stepped out of the doorway just as Garbo was entering; fixing her eyes on the pavement, Valentina, who never lacked for a dramatic gesture, shuddered and crossed herself.

*I* was thinking maybe I should get a new color scheme in here—I mean for the telephones. I only have black telephones. That'll keep me awake at night, trying to decide the color scheme. I do so little telephoning it really doesn't matter. Sometimes I don't call for weeks, anyone. . . . Still, every little bit of color counts. Maybe I would use the telephones more if they were bright. . . . I don't answer the telephone. Not because I don't hear it—I just don't answer it. It never rings at night, and when it rings during the daytime it's never answered anyway. I don't know who would be calling me, because I don't know anybody. Anyway, maybe I should change the colors—wouldn't that be funny? I like shocking pink most of all. But I can't imagine not having black telephones. We all become slaves to our possessions. I know people who live in a hotel, and they have a very valuable collection of paintings, and when they leave, they have the things taken out of the hotel. Anybody can come in with a latchkey, and off go the paintings.

You should be able to look at what you have, stare at it there when you want to, and if it goes, it goes. That's that.

The public was given a posthumous peek inside Garbo's home on September 2, 1990, in the *New York Times Magazine*. Accompanying the pictures was Gray Horan's remembrance of her great aunt. Although the access was unprecedented, the story was of the official-view variety, and the tableaux were essentially museum period rooms, lacking any human vibration. But this article had a purpose, as did a videotaped tour of the apartment shown on cable television at about the same time: the promotion of the Garbo estate auction, handled by Sotheby's. To the public, the surprise was that this pioneer of casual styles lived so formally, that Garbo, so fond of rusticating outside the city and so chicly at home on Cedric Gibbons's sleek, *moderne* sets at MGM, surrounded herself with such stylized European elegance. Except for an oddly placed toy or two, there was nothing particularly unusual or eccentric about the place. There were instead fine, traditional things—Ming and Meissen porcelain, brass-mounted cabinets, Savonnerie carpets, ormolu-and-crystal chandeliers, silk-upholstered tabourets—and Garbo arranged them just so, creating a comfortable home for herself, and a lovely stage for receiving her few visitors.

Besides her most intimate friends, the only people Garbo ever brought into her inner sanctum—her bedroom—were Billy Baldwin and his assistant, Edward Zajac. According to Baldwin, she'd wanted the walls painted just so, and demonstrated by holding a candle under a mulberry-colored silk lamp shade, saying, "I found it in a dining car in the first train I ever traveled on across Sweden." Baldwin got the color right, and said he deserved a Nobel Prize for the achievement. (Garbo paid his large fee in cash, something she often did for services.) He ultimately found his "strange and complicated" client to be "heartbreaking, because you wanted to be a warm friend, but she simply wouldn't let you."

Signs of colorful life did exist in Garbo's large collection of impressionist and other paintings. There were portraits and still

Garbo and Anders Randolph on one of Cedric Gibbons's sets for The Painted Veil. She was notoriously passionate about the art direction of her films, asking at the start of each new one, "What will it look like?"

lifes, and pictures of houses and flowers and dogs and birds. She bought the paintings at excellent prices and in sprees—three Renoirs in November of 1942, seven Jawlenskys the following year. "The walls burn with important but rakishly, wrongly hung paintings," Truman Capote presumed in his *faux* tour. The paintings in the collection were not particularly important, even the ones by great artists. That they sold well at auction, along with the furniture and objects, had less to do with their qualities as works of art than with the luster of their provenance.

*I* went back to the gallery today, and there was this painting. I mean a goofy painting. And I thought, "What's the matter with me?" I can't stand horror, and some of the pictures I buy are horror things. They stare at you.

The boss wasn't there, but a salesgirl told me the price, and I said, "Well, there's no discussing it." I don't like it anyway. It's really a goofy painting. It looks like a parrot. But I took it. I don't even sign for them. I take them home and hang them up. They trust me.

This was Saturday, and my girl came to work and said, "Don't tell me it's one of those again." And I said, "Yeah, it's one of those again." And she said, "Now really, you can't, Miss Garbo. What do you want these things staring at you for?" Then she said, "Anyway, you can't have it, it's tax time."

I took it back and told the owner I liked it but that it was too much. I didn't haggle. I just returned it. Then the gallery called back . . . and said they couldn't let it go for under so-and-so. The price is indecent, and I'm a lone woman. . . .

Oh well, maybe I'll get it. I don't know who the hell else would buy it. It's really very strange. I'll probably regret it. No: They're my colors. I do like it. They're my colors.

For the New York Sotheby auctions, held in November 1990, people lined up four-deep around the block, just as they had for Garbo premieres long ago. The object of all the attention would have wanted to retreat from the spectacle, but just as surely would have let out one of her long, low whistles at the $20.7 million that the auction realized. Garbo had spent virtually her entire life, particularly the last forty years of it, creating her refuge, maintaining her myth, and barricading herself from the public, which now was invited to examine her possessions. Although she had absconded with so many of her secrets and so much of her mystery intact (she apparently had even destroyed her career records, including the scripts and correspondence that would be of value to film scholars), Sotheby's was able to offer up the relics she couldn't take with her. It at first seemed that those of moderate means might be able to walk away with a prize—an enameled ashtray, a little watercolor by an unknown artist, a glass vase, or a book. But prices soared under the hammer, some to twenty times their estimates. A porcelain scent bottle in the form of a cone-hatted wizard might be considered a tzotschka by some, but not by those who bid it up to $18,000. An Albert André painting of an old woman sold for $187,000, against a preauction estimate of $40,000. What was regarded as the most important painting in Garbo's collection, Renoir's portrait of his nephew Edmond, went for $7 million. Another Renoir, of the artist's youngest son and his nurse, *Leontine et Coco*, sold for $5.7 million. The third Renoir, however, called *Confidence*, a picture of a woman whispering a secret to a man, did not generate a bid at its floor of $2 million and was taken off the block. Bonnard's *Cornpoppies* hammered down at $3.2 million; and Garbo's six Jawlenskys—the artist's fantastically colored "mystical heads," still lifes, and landscapes —brought a total of $1.8 million.

Fabulous prices also were paid for Garbo's Louis XV and XVI furniture. A beechwood Marquise, signed by N. Heurtaut, c. 1765, richly scrolled and carved with flowers and foliage, fetched more than twice its estimate, bringing $71,500. A pair of mid-eighteenth-century *fauteuils*, with leaf-carved cabriole legs, attributed to Jean-Baptiste Tilliard, sold for $88,000.

Among the more obscure and perhaps more telling lots were three small pictures:

■ *Platonic Love*, a brightly colored oil painting by Nils Asther— Garbo's friend and fellow Swede and actor—of two fanciful elephants, trunks intertwined. (In *Wild Orchids* Garbo and Asther ride elephants to their trysting ground.) Estimated at $150, it sold for $9,350.

■ Christian Bérard's ink portrait of his fellow stage designer Cecil Beaton sold for $12,100. That the picture still hung in Garbo's home may be evidence that she had forgiven Beaton, who died in 1980, for publishing his candid memoir of their friendship. Beaton claimed to have been Garbo's lover, though he may have been the kind of man to whom an invitation to touch a person's vertebrae—which he makes much of Garbo allowing him and only him to do—qualified as making love.

■ A small, flatly colored painting called *Embracing Couple* sold for $9,350, over an estimate of $500. The artist was Sven Gustafsson (misspelled, with one *s*, in the Sotheby's catalog)—Garbo's brother.

N ew Yorkers are so friendly in the snow. Did you go out today? I shouldn't have done it. I went out for only a few blocks and everything went—my mascara went, everything went. I couldn't stay out. But it's lovely.

Everyone is so friendly. We should always live in a cold climate. Someone put out their hand to me to help me over a snow drift. Even *I* helped a lady over a drift.

Do you realize we've had no snow in New York for years? Just little bits of things, this dirty mush. We don't have any snow anymore. I don't know who's keeping the snow.

D o you know someone sent me a Christmas tree? It's about four feet tall, doesn't smell nuttin', doesn't smell a thing. Trees only smell if you have living candles to heat them up a bit, but then you set the house on fire. You can't win these days.

I didn't dress it. I just put it over there. Isn't it pretty? Well, I had some lights, so I stuck them on it. The rest will stay naked. I won't look at it—it'll stay in there and I'll stay in here. Maybe we'll look at it tomorrow, but I mustn't promise or say anything, because the minute I promise something then it never comes. I mean everything at the time, but then I always back out. I know nothing about *mañana*. I never discuss *mañana*.

Imagine someone sending me a Christmas tree! Quite unnecessary.

Garbo with her
brother, Sven, on a
trip home to
Stockholm.

Anonymous gifts were not unknown to Garbo, though it had always been her practice to ignore tribute she received from fans. Her refusal to answer or even open fan mail was one more flagrant violation of the Hollywood way. Spotting Garbo with a bandaged foot—apparently a tennis injury—Louella Parsons snipped that she must have tripped over her bags of unanswered fan mail. But the star never reformed. Unless she knew the sender, packages addressed to her at 450 East Fifty-second Street went unopened, even when they piled up in a downstairs storage room during the Christmas season and around the time of her birthday.

When her presence at the Villa Cimbone was made known during her harrowing sojourn in Italy with Leopold Stokowski, Garbo was deluged with mail. As *The New Yorker* reported it, she was contemptuous of those who would not let her alone:

*Every day fifty or more letters for Miss Garbo, many of them registered, came to the villa. All were ordered to be thrown into the furnace without being opened: manuscripts, plays, books, poems, everything was put in the flames. Sometimes there were packages. One package contained a new brassiere, with the request that Miss Garbo wear it, sign it, and return it to the sender. . . .*

*[Then] a package too large to be burned unopened came and was unwrapped for destruction. It contained two Spanish shawls: one in colors—this was rather fine— and a handsome white one. The colored shawl Miss Garbo added to her limited luggage. When she was leaving, perhaps because she had no money to tip . . . Miss Garbo gave [the Swiss housekeeper] the white shawl. After Miss Garbo drove away, the housekeeper, in her room, unfolded the shawl to try it on, and a letter fell out. It was from a Sicilian baronessa, who declared that her family dated from the fourteenth century, that they were impoverished but had been able to go see Miss Garbo in a film in which she had exhibited much pity for those in trouble, that she was una grande artista and so must also be as compassionate as she was talented, that these two valuable shawls were the last of the noble family's worldly possessions, and that since the shawls had to be relinquished, they willed Miss Garbo to be the purchaser, at such price as her generous soul would elect. The housekeeper, thin-lipped, put the white shawl in a new package and in the folds put a note, saying she was returning the white shawl but that Miss Garbo had taken the colored shawl and gone off with it, no one knew where on earth to."*

Probably the most extravagant gesture ever made to Garbo by a stranger came from Edgar H. Donne, a Michigan farmer who left her his entire estate, including 160 acres of land, $700 in war bonds, $180 in U.S. postal savings bonds, and, as stated in his will, "all securities and jewelry . . . and cash in the bank." Donne, an Englishman who claimed to be a descendant of the poet John Donne, actually was the sort who might have appealed to his beneficiary: Described as a hermit, he lived in a small, four-chimneyed cabin and slept on an oak table. He had spurned an oil company's interest in his land, because, he said, "drilling would spoil my trees." His crush on Garbo was serious—he once bought himself a new suit and made a trip to Hollywood, intending to propose to her. When his subsequent love letters went unanswered, he accused the postmasters of conspiracy. But Donne held hope, adding in a proviso to his will that "if Greta Garbo becomes my wife, then [my property shall go] to Greta

*I*t's been at least ten years since I went out on New Year's Eve. Maybe I'll get a New Year's hat—maybe I have one somewhere. No, no—I've never had one. Bully, bully, oh, *dear*. Well, I'm glad somebody has a good time somewhere; it makes the evening better.

On New Year's I go to bed, and if I go to sleep, I go to sleep. If I don't, or if I wake up in the middle of the night, I say "Happy New Year, Miss Garbo."

Wintertime, snowfall, and the December holidays gave Garbo pleasant memories of home, but also could put her "off-key," as she described it, and cause real despair. At the end of the year, she seemed especially fragile.

*Y*es, yes, yes—/"One thing is certain, and the rest are lies,/The flower that once has bloomed and dies . . ." I won't finish the sentence. I stopped just in time. If I finished it . . . well, it's very sad, and Father Christmas is right around the corner.

So *what?* I just jump over the whole thing. I'm the same all the time, a restless soul in the midst of the whole bloody thing. I still went up one of our beats, toward Altman's, then down Fifth. One shouldn't be that way. But that's what surroundings do to one—and time, time, bloody old time.

It was very eerie today. It was snowing a little bit—a peculiar kind of snow—and little bits of rain.

I realized it was Christmas and I thought maybe that kept the people in, too. I thought if I could get over to Second or First Avenue, there will be people, but there weren't. I was scared and got going. I could have gotten a cab, but I was determined to walk. I don't know why, but I did. As long as no one molested me or said, "Stick 'em up." But there were no people on the street. It was scary. . . .

Why go up my old route *today* . . . what for? I don't know, but I did it, and that was my big event for Christmas.

But there is something in the air this time of year which is nice, it makes people a little more gay. It's sweet, I'm sure. I wish I could be that way, too. In Sweden they'd be decorating trees with candles and walking in pure snow. Now I'm a sour little man, but I could be out jumping around.

Ah, poor Miss G.—oh, dear. Merry Christmas, Merry Christmas.

If something happened to me over the weekend, no one would know. My girl doesn't come over the weekend. Nobody in the world would know. Nobody would know.

Garbo died on Easter Sunday, 1990.

Opposite: *Garbo by Clarence Bull.*

# ACKNOWLEDGMENTS

Thank you:

Don Bachardy, the Christopher Isherwood estate; Ned Comstock, Doheeny Library, University of Southern California; Sam Gill, the Herrick Library, Academy of Motion Picture Arts and Sciences; Ronald Grele, Oral History Room, Butler Library, Columbia University; Diane Lasek, Turner Program Services; The Walter Wanger Papers, State Historical Society of Wisconsin; Nick Wyman and John Dobson, the Clarence Brown Collection, University of Tennessee, Knoxville; The New York Public Library; The Museum of Modern Art Film Library.

Lew Ayres; Franci Beck; Eleanor Boardman d'Arrast; Marian (Mrs. Clarence) Brown; James Card; J. J. (Joe) Cohn; Eleanore Phillips Colt; Douglas Fairbanks, Jr.; Ruth Ford; Leatrice Fountain; Bill Frye; Ellen Graham; Sam Green; Tammy Grimes; Marit Gruson; Jane Gunther; Rachael Oestricher Haspel; Katharine Hepburn; Nancy de Herrera; Jean Howard; Ross Hunter; Barbara Kaster, Bowdoin College, Department of Film; Mary Anita Loos; Sam Marx; Leonard Stanley; Annette Tapert; Stephanie Wanger; Billy Wilder.

—Vance Muse

I owe an enormous debt to Vance Muse for his outstanding research, excellent interviews, and his guidance and insightful editing throughout the preparation and writing of this book. It was Vance who suggested the title, *Walking with Garbo.*

For his ideas and guidance in mounting this project and for continuous encouragement in all things relating to Garbo, I am particularly indebted to Executive Editor Richard Kot of HarperCollins Publishers, and to his able assistant, Sheila Gillooly. Richard's moral support was tremendously important and invaluable to decision making. Grateful acknowledgment is made of the generous help given by many persons, and my gratitude to all of them is enormous. For the creation and shaping of the book itself, I am forever indebted to Joel Avirom for his elegant design and layout and to Vincent Virga, who assembled the superb collection of photographs that are certainly key to this book.

I must also express my thanks to valued friends and colleagues with whom I discussed the manuscript at any time. They are John Otis Kirkpatrick, Kathleen Gee Hjerter, Dorothy McCullum, Karen Kuydendall, Steven Franden, Dave Oliphant, Dan Loveland, Harry Middleton, Liz Carpenter, George Eells, Aurand Harris, Dr. Richard P. Wunder, Kevin Brownlow, Barry Paris, Peter Jones, Sheila Benson, Emma-Stina Prescott, Ruth Ford, Don Breitinger, Dr. Betty Sue Flowers, Dr. Thomas F. Staley, Muffie Staley, William Luce, Patricia Billfaldt, Earl Blackwell, and the Academy of Motion Picture Arts and Sciences' Stacey Endres, Ernest Lehman, Bayard Bastedo, Howard Woolmer, and Robert Foshko.

Gwynedd Cannan, the excellent cataloguer of the David O. Selznick Collection at the Harry Ransom Humanities Research Center, University of Texas at Austin, never failed to make that facility's archive treasures available. In addition, thanks is given to L. Jeffrey Selznick and Selznick biographer David Thomson for their cooperation and permission to quote from the Selznick files. Dr. Ronald Grele, Director of the Columbia University Oral History Collection, paved the way for the Rouben Mamoulian and Lillian Gish interviews to be included. And to Lillian Gish, to whom *Walking with Garbo* is dedicated, I am most grateful for the generous time she gave me in our interview for the American Biography Project. Miss Gish's manager, James Frasher, made my interview with Miss Gish a most rewarding experience.

Also indispensable were the ongoing counsel of William M. Parrish and Nancy Ebe. Lynne Hurlbutt was indefatigable in the processing of legal correspondence.

And finally, to literary agent Eric Ashworth, of Donadio/Ashworth, who together with Vance Muse suggested the book project, I owe an enormous intellectual and personal debt. Eric not only provided encouragement and assistance; without him there would be no book.

—Raymond Daum